THE
Fresh
PASTA
COOKBOOK

KT-150-114

THE *Fresh* **PASTA** COOKBOOK

INTERNATIONAL RECIPES FOR ALL SEASONS

BRIDGET JONES

APPLE

A QUINTET BOOK

Published by The Apple Press
6 Blundell Street
London N7 9BH

Copyright © 1993 Quintet Publishing Limited.
All rights reserved. No part of this publication
may be reproduced, stored in a retrieval system
or transmitted in any form or by any means,
electronic, mechanical, photocopying,
recording or otherwise, without the permission
of the copyright holder.

Reprinted 1997

ISBN 1-85076-423-9

This book was designed and produced by
Quintet Publishing Limited
6 Blundell Street
London N7 9BH

Creative Director: Richard Dewing
Designer: Ian Hunt
Project Editor: Katie Preston
Editor: Diana Vowles
Photographer: Trevor Wood
Illustrator: Annie Ellis

Typeset in Great Britain by
Central Southern Typesetters, Eastbourne
Manufactured in Singapore by
Colour Trend (Pte) Limited
Printed in Hong Kong by Sing Cheong Printing Co. Ltd.

Contents

CHAPTER ONE

PASTA PERFECT
Every Time

*There is no great mystery involved in making simple, Italian-style pasta dough.
All it takes is a touch of muscle power for the kneading and rolling – unless, of
course, you have a pasta machine which will make light work of pounding the
ingredients to a smooth, pliable dough. It really is worth making your own dough,*

*if only for filled pasta such as tortellini and ravioli; apart from the variety of
fillings which you can introduce, home-made filled pasta is infinitely superior to
the average (or even slightly better) bought alternatives. Remember that you can
make a large batch of shapes when the mood takes you, fill them and freeze them
for future use.*

*The majority of the recipes in the chapters which follow do not necessarily need
home-made pasta. Every larger supermarket offers a range of fresh pasta shapes
which usually includes spirals or twists which you cannot make at home, egg
noodles, spaghetti, lasagne, paglia e fieno and fettucine. Flavoured pasta doughs
vary in quality – spinach dough (verdi) is popular and tastes good but some of the
herb-flavoured doughs taste inferior and, frankly, may ruin a good home-made*

*sauce! However, look out for Italian delicatessens offering good-quality
flavoured pasta and fresh gnocchi.*

*Oriental noodles and pasta dough are also available fresh from specialist
supermarkets. Fresh Chinese egg noodles, won ton wrappers and rice sticks have
a finer flavour than the dried types and they also freeze extremely well, so it is
worth seeking out a source and buying a large batch. I include a recipe for won
ton dough which is not difficult to make and is a versatile wrapper for many types
of dim sum (snacks); however, flipping and flinging dough to form the long
strands of fine egg noodles is definitely a specialist technique.*

*The making of pasta can be immensely satisfying in itself, quite apart from the
dividends it pays in the quality of the final dish – so don a large apron, scrub
down the work surface and discover just how relaxing a pasta-making session can be.*

EQUIPMENT

You do not need any special equipment for making pasta. A large area of work surface helps, but it is not essential as you can always roll the dough in two or more batches. A mixing bowl, spoon and rolling pin are the basics, and an extra-long rolling pin is useful (make sure an ordinary one does not have knobs at the ends as they indent the dough and make rolling out difficult). You may also wish to invest in some of the following:

Pastry Wheel A fluted pastry wheel for cutting out ravioli.

Ravioli Tray A small metal tray with round or square hollows. Lay a sheet of pasta over the tray, press it in neatly and spoon mixture into the hollows. Brush with egg, cover with a second sheet of dough and roll the top to seal before cutting out the ravioli.

Pasta Machine A small but heavy metal machine for rolling pasta. Fitted with plain rollers which can be set at different distances apart, this basic, inexpensive machine is terrific. Once the dough is briefly kneaded, rolling it through the machine several times on the widest setting will complete the kneading.

Set the rollers at the narrow width for rolling out sheets of dough or substitute cutting rollers to make noodles or spaghetti. A ravioli filler attachment makes very small, neat ravioli by feeding the pasta and filling through a hopper-like attachment.

Electric Pasta Machines Large, expensive machines are available for mixing, kneading, rolling and extruding pasta. Unless you are an avid pasta eater, this is an unlikely piece of equipment for the average domestic kitchen.

Pasta Dryer A small wooden rack on which to hang cut noodles or sheets of pasta as they are rolled out.

BELOW
Hand-turned pasta machine with attachments for filled pasta.

Dough Making

1 *Kneading pasta dough.*

2 *Rolling out pasta dough.*

3 *Pasta shapes made with biscuit cutters.*

PASTA-MAKING TECHNIQUES

Mixing and Kneading

Unlike pastry, pasta dough needs a firm hand and a positive approach to mixing and kneading. The dough will seem very dry and prone to crumbling at first but as you knead it, the oil and egg combine fully with the flour and the ingredients bind together.

1 Mix the ingredients in the bowl, using a spoon at first, then your hand.

2 Begin the kneading process in the bowl, bringing the dough together and "wiping" the bowl clean of any crumbs.

3 Turn the dough out on to a lightly floured, clean surface and knead it into a ball. Add a little flour to the work surface to prevent the dough sticking, but try to keep this to the minimum during kneading.

4 Once the dough has come together, knead it firmly and rhythmically, pressing it down and out in one movement, then pulling the edge of the dough back in towards the middle in the next movement. Keep turning the dough as you knead it, so that you work it around in a circle rather than constantly pressing and pulling one side. Keep the dough moving and it will not stick to the surface.

5 The dough is ready when it is smooth and warm. Wrap it in a polythene bag or cling film and set it aside for 15–30 minutes if possible before rolling it out.

Rolling Out

When rolling the dough, try to keep it in the shape you want to end up with. Press the dough flat, forming it into an oblong or square, then roll it out firmly. Lift and "shake out" the dough a few times initially to ensure it does not stick to the surface. As the dough becomes thinner you have to handle it more carefully to avoid splitting it. However, pasta dough is far more durable than pastry and the smoother it becomes as it is rolled, the tougher it is. It can be rolled out very thinly – until you can almost see through it – without breaking, but this is not essential for the majority of pasta dishes. Dust the surface under the dough with a little flour occasionally, as necessary, and dust the top, rubbing the flour over the dough with one hand. Continue rolling until the dough is thin and even – a common mistake is to leave the dough too thick, so that it becomes unpleasantly solid when cooked. For noodles, or pasta which is to be eaten plain or topped with sauce, try to roll out to the thickness of a piece of brown paper: this makes excellent noodles.

Make sure the surface under the dough is sifted with flour, then cover the dough completely with cling film and leave for 10 minutes. This relaxes the dough before cutting – it is not essential but does prevent the dough from shrinking as it is cut.

ABOVE
Fruit and vegetable stall in Pienza, Italy.

Cutting Pasta

You need a large, sharp knife and a large floured platter or tray on which to place the pasta (a clean roasting tin will do). Flour the dough lightly before cutting. Once cut, keep the pasta dusted with flour to prevent it sticking together. Pasta may be dried before cooking by hanging it on a rack or spreading it out. I have, before now, draped pasta between two chair backs (covering them with kitchen paper first). Quite honestly, I have not found any great advantage to drying the pasta and have always felt that it is thoroughly inconvenient and unhygienic. It seems to cook well if it is added to boiling water straight after rolling.

Sheets Trim the dough edges so that they are straight, then cut the pasta into squares or oblongs. This is basic lasagne, so cut the dough to suit the size of dish.

Noodles Dust the dough well with flour, then roll it up. Use a sharp knife to cut the roll into 5 mm/ ¼ in wide slices. Shake out the slices as they are cut and they fall into long noodles. Keep the noodles floured and loosely piled on the tray to prevent them from sticking together. Cover loosely with cling film.

Circles or shapes Use biscuit cutters and aspic cutters to stamp out circles and shapes.

Squares Trim the dough edges, then use a clean, long ruler to cut the dough into wide strips. Cut these across into squares.

Small squares Use a ruler to cut the dough into 2.5 cm/1 in wide strips, then cut these across into squares. The small squares may be cooked and treated as bought pasta shapes.

Other shapes If you have the time, you can make other shapes by hand. Cut the dough into strips, then into small oblongs or squares. By twisting, pleating or pinching you can make bows and funny little twists and, I am sure, lots of clever alternatives. Frankly, I feel inclined to leave this to the manufacturers as it is very time-consuming.

LEFT
Home-made fresh pasta squares.

RIGHT
Home-made fresh pasta bows.

Cooking Fresh Pasta

Pasta should be cooked in enormous quantities of boiling water. Although you can get away with less water than the volume which is always suggested for authentic recipes (which means using a stock pot or catering-size pan when cooking enough for four people), you need a large saucepan which holds 3.4–3.9 litres/6–7 pt to cook 350–450 g/12–16 oz pasta. If you have a stock pot or very large pressure cooker which you can use without the lid on, so much the better.

Pour water into the pan to three-quarters of its capacity. Add salt and bring the water to the boil. Adding a little oil to the water helps to prevent it from frothing on the surface and boiling over rapidly – the pasta will not stick together if you have a pan which is large enough, and adding oil does little to prevent the pasta sticking in a pan which is too small! Add the pasta when the water is fully boiling, give it a stir and bring the water back to the boil rapidly. Be ready to reduce the heat otherwise the water will froth over. Cook for about 3 minutes for noodles and other types of unfilled pasta. Filled pasta requires longer to allow the filling to cook through.

When cooked, the pasta should be "al dente" (with bite). It should be firm yet tender, not soft or sticky. Drain the cooked pasta at once, pouring it into a large colander. Shake the colander over the sink, then tip the pasta into a hot bowl and add the dressing or sauce. Serve at once.

Chilling Prepared Pasta

Dust the pasta with plenty of flour and place it in a large airtight container in the refrigerator. Cook within 2 days of making or freeze promptly. The unrolled dough may be wrapped and chilled for 1–2 days.

Leftover Cooked Pasta

Cool quickly and chill in a covered container. Reheat pasta in the microwave or in a sauce on the hob or in the oven.

Freezing Pasta

Uncooked fresh pasta freezes very well but it is best to roll and cut the dough first. Separate sheets of pasta by interleaving freezer film between them. Flour noodles and pack them loosely in polythene bags, then spread them out fairly flat for freezing, so they do not form a lump. Bought fresh pasta is an excellent freezer candidate which is ideal for impromptu meals.

Do not thaw frozen pasta before cooking, simply add it to boiling water and cook as for fresh pasta. Noodles and most other shapes take about the same time to cook as unfrozen pasta, once the water has come to the boil again. Frozen filled pasta requires extra cooking time to allow the filling to thaw and cook properly.

Cooked lasagne and cannelloni or similar layered pasta dishes freeze well but cooked shapes and noodles tend to have an inferior texture if frozen after cooking.

USING THE RECIPES

☛ Use either metric or Imperial quantities, not a mixture of both as they are not interchangeable.

☛ All spoon measures refer to standard measuring spoons. Do not use table cutlery as the volume will vary. Quantities refer to level measuring spoons.

tbsp = tablespoon   tsp = teaspoon

☛ Oven temperatures refer to conventional ovens; if you have a forced convection oven, please refer to the manufacturer's instructions for adapting cooking times or temperatures.

☛ Unless otherwise stated, herbs are fresh, not dried.

☛ Eggs are size 3 unless otherwise stated.

RIGHT
Traditional Italian ham and wines at a restaurant in Monte Reggiano, Tuscany.

RIGHT
Fresh pasta noodles ready for freezing.

Pasta Dough

MAKES ABOUT 600 G/1 ¼ LB PASTA

350 g/12 oz strong plain flour
1 tsp salt
3 eggs
4 tbsp olive oil
1 tbsp water

Mix the flour and salt together in a large bowl. Make a well in the middle, then add the eggs, olive oil and water. Use a spoon to mix the eggs, oil and water, gradually working in the flour. When the mixture begins to bind into clumps, scrape the spoon clean and knead the dough together with your hands.

Press the dough into a ball and roll it around the bowl to leave the bowl completely clean of the mixture. Then turn the dough out on a lightly floured, clean surface and knead it thoroughly until it is smooth. Follow the notes on kneading (see page 9), keeping the dough moving and adding the minimum extra flour required to prevent it sticking as you work. Wrap the dough in a polythene bag and leave it to rest for 15–30 minutes before rolling it out. Do not chill the dough as this will make it difficult to handle.

Mixing the dough.

Flavoured Pasta

The following may be used with the above recipe.

Beetroot Purée 50 g/2 oz cooked and peeled beetroot with 2 eggs in a food processor or liquidizer, or press it through a sieve (this eliminates dark speckles). Add the beetroot purée with the remaining egg. Omit the oil and water. Do not use beetroot which has been preserved in acetic acid or vinegar: it must be freshly boiled or the untreated vacuum-packed type.

Carrot Omit half the oil and water but add 2 tbsp carrot juice with the eggs. Natural carrot juice is available from wholefood shops and delicatessens.

Herb Add 4 tbsp chopped mixed fresh herbs to the flour and salt. Suitable herbs include parsley, thyme, sage, tarragon, chives, chervil, marjoram and fennel. Rosemary may be used but only in very small quantities as it is a strongly flavoured herb. Balance the delicate herbs against the stronger ones by using less of the latter. Use two, three or more herbs but remember that a delicate herb like dill will be totally lost if combined with many other herbs. Dill is best mixed with chives and a little parsley.

Olive Finely chop 100 g/4 oz black olives and add them to the flour.

Spinach Wash and trim 225 g/8 oz fresh spinach. Place the damp leaves in a saucepan. Cover tightly and cook over high heat for 5 minutes, shaking the pan often. Turn the spinach into a sieve placed over a basin. Press and squeeze all the juice from the spinach, leaving the leaves as dry as possible. Add 6 tbsp spinach juice to the pasta and omit the oil and water.

Tomato Add 1 tbsp concentrated tomato purée, beating it into the eggs.

Turmeric Add 1 tsp ground turmeric to the flour. For a pleasing, unusual, lightly spiced pasta, add 1 tbsp white cumin seeds to the flour with the turmeric.

Walnut Use walnut oil instead of olive oil.

Won Ton Dough

MAKES ABOUT 350 G/12 OZ DOUGH

175 g/6 oz plain flour
50 g/2 oz cornflour
pinch of salt
1 egg, beaten
100 ml/4 fl oz water

Sift the flour, cornflour and salt into a bowl, then make a well in the middle. Add the egg and pour in the water. Use a spoon to mix the egg and water into the flour. When the mixture binds together, scrape the spoon clean and use your hand to work the dough into a smooth ball, leaving the bowl free of mixture.

Turn the dough out on a clean surface and knead it thoroughly until it is very smooth. Cut the dough in half and wrap both portions in polythene or cling film, then set aside for 15–30 minutes.

Roll out one portion of dough at a time. Dust the work surface and rolling pin lightly with cornflour, then roll out the dough as required until it is thin and even.

When rolling out the dough for won tons, try to keep it in a square shape, then trim the edges. Use a clean, long ruler as a guide for cutting the dough in wide strips, then cut in the opposite direction to make squares.

Alternatively, a plain round biscuit cutter may be used to stamp rounds out of the dough for making various dim sum, such as dumplings and packets.

CHAPTER TWO

PASTA SIMPLE
In its Prime

The difference between fresh and dried pasta is most noticeable when it plays a prime role in a dish, with the minimum of additional ingredients. The recipes in this chapter highlight the ease of serving up a simple pasta meal that delights the palate — the right mix of herbs or spices, a little fruit here and the tang of cheese there, or favourite everyday ingredients combined with satisfying success. Many of these dishes are quick to make and especially easy to serve. A few

large, colourful bowls are by far the best dishes in which to serve pasta, particularly these "throw-it-all-in" recipes. If you want to offer accompaniments, remember that old favourites are often the best: a good green salad and some warmed crusty bread are quite sufficient and often superfluous anyway, except for very hungry horses!

Pasta with Oil and Garlic

Good-quality olive oil and plump fresh garlic turn a plate of fresh pasta into a positive feast of a snack! You can increase the quantities of oil and garlic to suit your taste and serve with freshly grated parmesan if you like.

SERVES 4

100–150 ml/4–5 fl oz olive oil
4 garlic cloves, chopped
freshly ground black pepper
450 g/1 lb tagliatelle or spaghetti

Heat the oil and garlic in a small saucepan. Cook the garlic very gently for 2 minutes – it should not fry rapidly, simply give up its flavour to the oil. Toss the oil and garlic and freshly ground black pepper into the drained pasta. Serve at once.

Pasta with Butter and Parmesan

SERVES 4

75 g/3 oz butter

75 g/3 oz freshly grated parmesan cheese

450 g/1 lb pasta

freshly ground black pepper

Soften the butter, then gradually mix in the parmesan cheese and beat the mixture until it is soft and creamy. Dot it over the drained pasta, then toss well and add freshly ground black pepper to taste. Serve at once.

Spaghetti with Walnuts and Olives

SERVES 4

75 ml/3 fl oz olive oil

knob of butter

1 garlic clove, crushed (optional)

175 g/6 oz walnuts, finely chopped

100 g/4 oz black olives, roughly chopped

2 tbsp capers, chopped

4 tbsp chopped parsley

freshly ground black pepper

450 g/1 lb spaghetti

Heat the oil and butter with the garlic (if using) until the butter melts. Stir in the walnuts, cook gently for 2 minutes, then add the olives, capers, parsley, a little salt and plenty of freshly ground black pepper. Pour the mixture over the drained spaghetti, toss well and serve at once.

BELOW
The beautiful area called Crete, south of Siena, Italy.

RIGHT
Spaghetti with Walnuts and Olives.

Tagliatelle with Chick Peas and Basil

Pasta and chick peas are two of my favourite supper foods – with aromatic fresh basil, this is a wonderful combination.

SERVES 4

4 tbsp olive oil

1 garlic clove, crushed

6 tbsp snipped chives

4 sage leaves, chopped

salt and freshly ground black pepper

2 × 400 g/14 oz cans chick peas, drained

450 g/1 lb tagliatelle verdi

6 basil sprigs

Heat the olive oil, garlic, chives, sage, salt and freshly ground black pepper with the chick peas in a large saucepan for about 3 minutes. The idea is to heat the ingredients rather than to cook them. Add the drained pasta and toss well. Leave the pan over the lowest heat setting while you use scissors to shred the basil sprigs over the pasta, discarding any tough stalk ends. Mix lightly and serve.

Spirals with Grapes and Goat's Cheese

This is delicious for a light lunch or as a starter. Serve with slices of French bread.

SERVES 4

2 slices round chèvre goat's cheese, each cut in 8 small wedges

175 g/6 oz seedless green grapes

2 bunches of watercress, trimmed and roughly shredded

4 spring onions, chopped

grated rind and juice of 1 orange

4 tbsp olive oil

salt and freshly ground black pepper

350 g/12 oz pasta spirals

Mix the cheese, grapes, watercress and spring onions in a large bowl. Pour in the orange rind and juice and olive oil, then add a little salt and plenty of freshly ground black pepper. Mix well. Divide the hot, freshly drained pasta between four serving plates, then top each with a quarter of the cheese mixture. Serve at once.

Sun-dried Tomato and Vermouth Special

You can keep a jar of the dressing in the fridge for a couple of weeks for emergency pasta snacks!

SERVES 4

12 sun-dried tomatoes
175 ml/6 fl oz dry white vermouth
1 bay leaf
1 large marjoram sprig
100 ml/4 fl oz olive oil
450 g/1 lb small pasta squares (page 14), spirals or broken spaghetti
freshly ground black pepper
1 red or white onion, very thinly sliced and separated into rings
freshly grated parmesan cheese, to serve

Use a pair of kitchen scissors to snip the tomatoes into strips, then across into small pieces. Do this over a large screw-top jar. Add the vermouth, bay leaf and marjoram, then pour in the oil and cover the jar. Shake well and leave to stand for at least 3 hours – the longer the better, ideally overnight.

Tip the tomato mixture into a small saucepan and heat fairly slowly until just boiling. Reduce the heat so that the mixture barely bubbles and leave while you cook the pasta. Stir the tomatoes occasionally, then stir well just before pouring over the piping hot, drained pasta. Add the freshly ground black pepper and toss the pasta to coat all the pieces with the dressing. Top with the fine onion rings and serve with parmesan cheese.

COOK'S TIP

Dried marjoram is too harsh for the sauce. If you do not have any fresh marjoram, add a very small sprig of thyme or a sage sprig instead. Onions with red or white skins have a mild flavour which makes them ideal for eating raw. I like the contrast between the crisp, zingy onion and the rather sultry dried tomato dressing.

Pasta with Ham and Two Peppers

SERVES 4

2 tbsp dried red peppercorns, coarsely crushed
2 tbsp dried green peppercorns, coarsely crushed
4 tbsp chopped parsley
4 tbsp snipped chives
½ cucumber, peeled
2 tsp chopped mint (optional)
450 g/1 lb pasta
50 g/2 oz butter
350 g/12 oz lean cooked ham, finely shredded

Mix the red and green peppercorns, parsley and chives. Cut the cucumber into 2.5 cm/1 in lengths, then slice these pieces vertically and cut the slices into fine strips. Mix the mint into the cucumber strips.

While the pasta is cooking, melt the butter. Toss the hot butter and the ham into the drained pasta. Sprinkle the peppercorn mixture over and toss lightly. Top each portion with shredded cucumber and serve at once.

LEFT

Sun-dried Tomato and Vermouth Special.

Asparagus Supreme

This is really simple and quite unbeatable, especially if you are able to raid a pick-your-own farm for the freshest possible asparagus and cook the vegetable while it still spits with zest as you snap the spears. If you are having a healthy spell, toss the asparagus in 1 tablespoon hot olive oil and mix some fromage frais into the pasta instead of using lots and lots of butter!

SERVES 4

450 g/1 lb asparagus, trimmed of woody ends if necessary

75 g/3 oz butter

salt and freshly ground black pepper

450 g/1 lb tagliatelle verdi or spinach-flavoured small pasta squares (page 14)

3 tbsp chopped fresh dill

freshly grated parmesan cheese, to serve (optional)

Cook the asparagus in boiling salted water for 10–20 minutes, until just tender. If you do not have a tall asparagus saucepan, use the deepest pan you have and put the asparagus in it so that the tips stand above the rim. Tent foil over the top of the pan, crumpling it securely around the rim to seal in the steam. Very fresh, young asparagus will cook in 10 minutes, larger or more mature spears take longer.

Heat the butter while the pasta is cooking. Drain the asparagus and cut the spears into short lengths, then add them to the butter. Add a little seasoning, then pour the asparagus mixture over the drained pasta. Sprinkle with dill and mix well. Serve at once, with freshly grated parmesan if you like.

Spaghetti with Smoked Sausage and Carrots

A good, inexpensive and satisfying supper dish: the sweetness of the carrot complements the flavoursome sausage. Try to find smoked sausage made with fresh garlic.

SERVES 4

3 tbsp olive oil

1 onion, halved and thinly sliced

225 g/8 oz carrots, coarsely grated

450 g/1 lb smoked sausage, cut into strips

salt and freshly ground black pepper

450 g/1 lb spaghetti

50 g/2 oz butter

Heat the oil in a large frying pan. Add the onion and cook for 5 minutes, then add the carrots and sausage. Cook, stirring often, for about 10 minutes, until the pieces of sausage are browned in parts and the carrots are lightly cooked. Add seasoning to taste. Add the butter to the carrot and sausage mixture, toss the lot into the drained spaghetti and serve at once.

Fresh Green Pasta

This combination of ingredients also makes an excellent salad. If you use very small pasta squares, the hot mixture may also be served in scooped-out tomatoes as a first course.

SERVES 4

225 g/8 oz shelled or frozen peas
4 tbsp olive oil or 50 g/2 oz butter
4 spring onions, chopped
2 avocados, halved and cut into chunks
juice of 1/2 lemon
salt and freshly ground black pepper
450 g/1 lb pasta verdi
1 tbsp chopped mint
mint sprigs to garnish (optional)

Cook the peas in boiling salted water for 10 minutes. Heat the oil or melt the butter in a saucepan. Add the spring onions and cook for 1 minute, then stir in the peas, avocado and lemon juice. Season to taste.

Toss the pea and avocado mixture into the drained pasta. Sprinkle the mint over and serve at once. Mint sprigs may be added as a garnish if liked.

Egg and Tomato Favourite

Familiar foods that go together well make this slightly unusual yet reassuring supper dish.

SERVES 4

450 g/1 lb tomatoes, peeled and roughly chopped (see Cook's Tip)
salt and freshly ground black pepper
4 tbsp chopped parsley
8 eggs
large knob of butter
450 g/1 lb pasta
freshly grated parmesan or Cheddar cheese, to serve

Place the tomatoes in a basin and season them well, then mix in the parsley. Place the eggs in a saucepan, cover with cold water and bring to the boil. Cook for 10 minutes, then drain. Shell the eggs under cold water so as not to burn your fingers and place them in a basin, then cut them into eighths.

Toss the hot eggs and butter into the pasta, then mix in the tomatoes when the butter has melted. Serve at once, topping each portion with grated cheese.

COOK'S TIP

To peel tomatoes, place them in a bowl and pour boiling water over them. Leave to stand for 30–60 seconds: ripe tomatoes are ready quickly, under-ripe fruit may require an extra 30 seconds. Split the skins with a sharp, pointed knife and they will rub off easily.

Tagliatelle with Sesame Cabbage

Herb-flavoured tagliatelle is ideal for this recipe.

SERVES 4

4 tbsp sunflower oil
1 large onion, chopped
1 garlic clove, crushed
3 tbsp sesame seeds
3 tbsp currants
salt and freshly ground black pepper
450 g/1 lb red or white cabbage, shredded
1 tbsp cider vinegar
450 g/1 lb tagliatelle

Heat the oil, then add the onion, garlic, sesame seeds and currants. Add seasoning to taste. Cook, stirring often, over moderate to low heat for about 20 minutes, until the onion is well cooked. Stir in the cabbage and cook for about 10 minutes, stirring often, so that the cabbage is lightly cooked and still crunchy. Add the cider vinegar and stir well.

Toss the cabbage mixture with the freshly drained tagliatelle and serve at once.

Smoked Tofu with Squares

Pasta flavoured with herbs or tomatoes goes very well with smoked tofu. If you do not want to make your own pasta, buy fresh spirals or paglia e fieno.

SERVES 4

2 tbsp olive oil
25 g/1 oz butter
4 celery sticks, finely diced
1 green pepper, seeded and diced
salt and freshly ground black pepper
450 g/1 lb smoked tofu, cut into small cubes
grated rind of 1 lemon
2 spring onions, finely chopped
3 tbsp chopped parsley
450 g/1 lb small pasta squares (page 14)
lemon wedges, to serve

Heat the oil and butter in a large saucepan. Add the celery and cook, stirring, for 5 minutes. Add the green pepper, a little salt and plenty of freshly ground black pepper, stir well and cook gently for a further 10 minutes. Lightly mix the tofu into the pepper and celery, then leave to heat through for about 5 minutes.

Mix the lemon rind, spring onions and parsley. Toss the drained pasta with the tofu mixture and serve in individual bowls. Sprinkle with the lemon rind, spring onion and parsley mixture and serve with lemon wedges. The juice from the lemon may be squeezed over the pasta.

BELOW
The Ponte Vecchio in Florence.

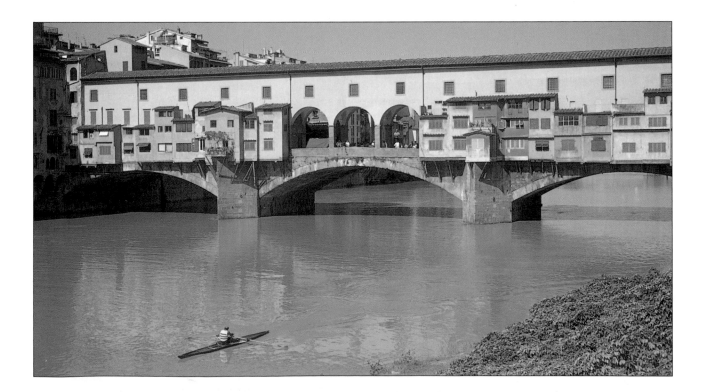

Pasta with Eggs and Tarragon

An easy dish that makes a tasty change from poached eggs on toast! Serve half portions for a starter or light snack.

SERVES 4

75 g/3 oz butter (or use olive oil or a mixture of butter and olive oil if preferred)

3 tbsp chopped tarragon

8 eggs

450 g/1 lb pasta (tagliatelle, paglia e fieno or spirals)

freshly ground black pepper

freshly grated parmesan cheese, to serve

Warm four plates or bowls. Melt the butter (or heat the oil with the butter if used) and add the tarragon, then set aside over very low heat. Poach the eggs when the pasta is just ready for draining.

Divide the pasta between the plates or bowls. Place a couple of eggs on each portion, then spoon the butter and tarragon over the top. Season with black pepper and serve at once with grated parmesan cheese.

Pasta with Mixed Mushrooms

SERVES 4

25 g/1 oz dried mushrooms
300 ml/½ pt dry white wine
50 g/2 oz butter
225 g/8 oz chestnut mushrooms, sliced
225 g/8 oz oyster mushrooms, sliced
300 ml/½ pt single cream
salt and freshly ground black pepper
3 tbsp chopped parsley
450 g/1 lb pasta
freshly grated parmesan cheese, to serve

Place the dried mushrooms in a basin and pour the wine over them. Cover with a saucer and weight it down to keep the mushrooms submerged in the wine. Leave for 30 minutes. Discard any tough stalks and slice the mushrooms if necessary (they are usually sold sliced in packets).

Melt the butter in a large saucepan. Add the chestnut mushrooms and cook for 5 minutes, stirring, then pour in the dried mushrooms and wine from soaking. Bring to the boil, reduce the heat and cook at a steady simmer for 15 minutes. Stir in the oyster mushrooms, cook for 2–3 minutes, then add the cream, seasoning and parsley. Heat gently, stirring, but do not boil or the sauce will curdle.

Add the drained pasta to the sauce, remove from the heat and mix well. Allow to stand, covered, for 2–3 minutes, then toss the pasta again and serve with grated parmesan cheese.

Pasta Carbonara

SERVES 4

50 g/2 oz butter

350 g/12 oz cooked ham, shredded

8 eggs

salt and freshly ground black pepper

150 ml/¼ pt single cream

450 g/1 lb tagliatelle

plenty of chopped parsley

freshly grated parmesan cheese, to serve

BELOW
*Looking across the Tuscan hills
from San Gimignano.*

Melt the butter in a large, heavy-bottomed or non-stick saucepan. Add the ham and cook for 2 minutes. Beat the eggs with seasoning and the cream. Reduce the heat under the pan, if necessary, then pour in the eggs and cook them gently, stirring all the time until they are creamy. Do not cook the eggs until they set and scramble and do not increase the heat to speed up the process or the carbonara will be spoilt.

The pasta should be added to the boiling water at the same time as adding the eggs to the pan. This way, the pasta will be drained and hot, ready to be tipped into the eggs. When the eggs are half set, add the pasta, mix well until the eggs are creamy and serve at once, sprinkled with parsley. Offer parmesan cheese with the pasta carbonara.

CHAPTER THREE

DRESSINGS AND SAUCES
For Fresh Pasta

It is very difficult to select a group of sauces for such an essential chapter because there are so many possibilities that the list can become endless. I have included the basic recipes which are often used in composite pasta dishes – a meat ragout, a tomato sauce and a selection of milk-based sauces; there are also other familiar sauce recipes which make versatile standbys. However, in addition, you will find a good selection of different sauces to surprise the taste buds.

Remember that many sauces freeze well, so it can be worth having a batch-cooking session, both for making fresh pasta and for preparing the sauces. Tomato sauce, in particular, is really worth making in quantity *when tomatoes are either inexpensive or good flavour-wise.*

Look out for plum tomatoes, as they make excellent sauces. There are suggestions about the choice of pasta in some recipes; apart from the practicalities of what you feel like making or the range of fresh pasta in your local supermarket, think about the shape of the pasta and the texture of the sauce when you are looking for the perfect match.

Big, chunky sauces can be difficult to eat with long, fine pasta such as spaghetti, and very small pasta shapes can be lost with either a thin sauce or a chunky one. This may seem to be a minor point, yet it is strange how shape and size can alter the balance of the dish and impair the enjoyment of it. In the absence of a vast variety, good old ribbon noodles, tagliatelle or fettucine as they may be called, taste good with most sauces!

Cardamom Fish Sauce

Lemon and coriander pep up plain white fish in this delicious sauce. It is particularly good with spirals or small pieces of pasta, such as squares or cut-up spaghetti; saffron or turmeric pasta is ideal if you are making your own. For a first course, serve half quantities of sauce in small rings of saffron or turmeric noodles.

SERVES 4

25 g/1 oz butter
1 small onion, finely chopped
1 red pepper, seeded and diced
6 green cardamoms
1 bay leaf
grated rind of 1 lemon
25 g/1 oz plain flour
300 ml/1/2 pt fish stock
salt and freshly ground black pepper
675 g/1 1/2 lb white fish fillet, skinned and cut into chunks
300 ml/1/2 pt single cream
2 tbsp chopped coriander leaves

Melt the butter in a saucepan. Add the onion, pepper, cardamoms, bay leaf and lemon rind. Press the cardamoms to split them slightly, then cook gently for 20 minutes, until the onion and pepper are well cooked. Stir often, so that the bay and spices give up their flavour and the onions do not brown.

Stir in the flour, then gradually pour in the stock, stirring all the time, and bring to the boil. Reduce the heat, if necessary, so that the sauce just simmers – it will be too thick at this stage. Add seasoning and the fish. Stir lightly, then cover the pan and cook gently for 20 minutes, or until the fish is cooked. Gently stir in the cream, then heat through without boiling. Taste for seasoning before serving sprinkled with the coriander.

Salmon with Dill and Mustard

Although delicate, salmon is a rich fish and the piquancy of this mustard sauce complements it perfectly. For classic simplicity, arrange the fish and its dressing on home-made egg noodles; or add a zesty note to the pasta by mixing the grated rind of 1 lemon with the flour when mixing the dough. The dill must be fresh – forget the recipe when you only have dried dill as it will make the sauce taste as though you have used grass cuttings.

SERVES 4

675–900 g/1½–2 lb salmon fillet, skinned
salt and freshly ground black pepper
4 tbsp olive oil
1 tbsp lemon juice
½ onion, finely chopped
2 tbsp flour
150 ml/¼ pt milk
4 tbsp Dijon mustard or other mild mustard
300 ml/½ pt soured cream
3 tbsp chopped dill
¼ cucumber, peeled and finely diced
1 celery stick, finely diced

Lay the salmon on a large piece of double-thick foil. Season it really well, then sprinkle with 1 tablespoon of the oil and the lemon juice. Grill the fish for about 15 minutes, or until cooked through.

Meanwhile, heat the remaining oil in a saucepan and add the onion. Cook, stirring, for 10 minutes. Stir in the flour and cook for 3 minutes before stirring in the milk, then bring to the boil. Beat the mustard into the thick sauce, then stir in the cream and heat gently but do not boil. Finally, stir in the dill and remove from the heat, then taste for seasoning.

Mix the cucumber and celery. Drain the cooking liquid from the salmon into the sauce. Use two forks to separate the cooked salmon into large chunks. Mix the mustard and dill sauce into the pasta, then lightly mix in the fish. Divide between serving platters and top each portion with a little of the cucumber and celery.

COOK'S TIP

Fresh dill freezes well for use in sauces but it will not retain its shape for garnishing. The herb thaws quickly and becomes limp; however, it crushes easily in its packet while frozen, separating the stalks from the fine fronds. If crushed and measured while frozen, the dill will not need chopping.

Anchovy and Egg Cream Sauce

This sauce is quick to prepare for unexpected guests, especially if you keep cream in the freezer. Good with spaghetti, noodles or shapes and ideal, in small quantities, for a first course.

SERVES 4

8 eggs
50 g/2 oz can anchovy fillets
4 spring onions, chopped
300 ml/1/2 pt single cream
freshly ground black pepper
plenty of shredded basil or chopped parsley

Place the eggs in a saucepan and cover with cold water. Bring to the boil, then cook for 8 minutes. Meanwhile, drain the oil from the anchovies into a small pan. Add the onions and cook for 2 minutes. Chop the anchovy fillets, add them to the onions, then stir in the cream and add pepper to taste. Heat very gently but do not allow to simmer or the cream will curdle.

Shell and roughly chop the eggs, then mix them into the sauce with basil or parsley. Serve at once, tossed into the hot pasta.

Tonnato Dressing

Tonnato is a cold sauce which is traditionally served with cold cooked veal; however, this versatile tuna mayonnaise is excellent on freshly cooked pasta of any type – try making olive-flavoured noodles and serve them as a first course topped with this sauce. The sauce is also good tossed with cold cooked pasta and served on a green salad base to make a tempting cocktail.

SERVES 4

2 egg yolks
juice of 1 lemon
salt and freshly ground black pepper
200 g/7 oz can tuna in oil
200 ml/7 fl oz olive oil
150 ml/1/4 pt soured cream, fromage frais or Greek-style yogurt (optional)
2 tbsp capers, chopped
chopped parsley, to serve

Place the egg yolks in a bowl. Use an electric beater to whisk in the lemon juice and a little seasoning. Whisk in the oil drained from the can of tuna. Whisking all the time on high speed, trickle in the olive oil very slowly. If you add the oil too quickly, the mixture will curdle; however, once it begins to thicken into a creamy mayonnaise, the oil can be poured in more quickly.

Mash the tuna fish to a paste, then mix it into the mayonnaise. Stir in the cream, fromage frais or yogurt (if used) and the capers. (The cream, fromage frais or yogurt lighten the sauce slightly.) Taste for seasoning before serving and sprinkle the pasta and sauce with chopped parsley.

COOK'S TIP

Cheating is invited here! Use 300 ml/1/2 pt good-quality mayonnaise (not the cheaper, acidic type) instead of making your own. Alternatively, for a low-fat version, mash the tuna and stir in a mixture of low-fat soft cheese and fromage frais.

Piquant Prawn and Tomato Sauce

Good with spaghetti or noodles, this sauce may also be layered with lasagne, then covered with a creamy topping and baked.

SERVES 4

2 tbsp oil
2 garlic cloves, crushed
2 green chillies, seeded and chopped
1 large onion, chopped
1 green pepper, seeded and diced
1 carrot, diced
2 celery sticks, diced
1 bay leaf
2 × 400 g/14 oz cans chopped tomatoes
1 tbsp tomato purée
1 tsp sugar
salt and freshly ground black pepper
450 g/1 lb frozen peeled cooked prawns
2 tbsp chopped coriander leaves

Heat the oil in a large saucepan. Add the garlic, chillies, onion, green pepper, carrot, celery and bay leaf. Cook, stirring, for 20 minutes. Then stir in the tomatoes, tomato purée, sugar and plenty of seasoning. Bring to the boil, reduce the heat, cover and simmer gently for 30 minutes.

Add the prawns, stir well and cook for 15 minutes, or until they are hot through. Taste for seasoning, then ladle the sauce over the pasta and top with the coriander.

Seafood Medley

You can vary the mixture of seafood according to your budget, the choice at the fishmongers and personal preference. Remember to add delicate ingredients at the end so they do not overcook. Serve with plain pasta or try combining a mixture of tomato, spinach and plain pasta.

SERVES 4

900 g/2 lb mussels
1 bay leaf
300 ml/½ pt dry white wine
6 tbsp olive oil
1 onion, halved and thinly sliced
1 celery stick, finely diced
1 green pepper, seeded and finely diced
3 garlic cloves, crushed
grated rind of 1 lemon
salt and freshly ground black pepper
4 small squid, cleaned and sliced
350 g/12 oz monkfish fillet, cut in small chunks
6–8 scallops, shelled and sliced
350 g/12 oz peeled cooked prawns, thawed if frozen
8 black olives, pitted and chopped
plenty of chopped parsley
freshly grated parmesan cheese, to serve

Scrub the mussels and scrape off any barnacles or dirt on the shell. Pull away the black beard which protrudes from the shell. Discard any open mussels which do not shut when tapped. Place the mussels in a large pan and add the bay leaf and wine. Bring the wine to the boil, then put a close-fitting lid on the pan and reduce the heat slightly so that the

Seafood Medley.

wine does not boil too rapidly. Cook for about 10 minutes, shaking the pan often, until the mussels are all open. Strain the mussels, reserving the cooking liquor and bay leaf. Reserve a few mussels in shells for garnish, if you like, and use a fork to remove the others from their shells.

Heat the oil in a large saucepan. Add the reserved bay leaf, onion, celery, green pepper, garlic, lemon rind and plenty of seasoning. Cover and cook, stirring occasionally, for 20 minutes, or until the onion is softened but not browned. Pour in the liquor from the mussels, bring to the boil and boil hard for about 3 minutes, or until reduced by half. Then reduce the heat and add the squid. Cover the pan and simmer for 5 minutes. Add the monkfish, cover the pan again and cook for a further 5 minutes. Next, add the scallops and cook gently for 3 minutes, or until the seafood is just cooked.

Add the prawns, mussels and olives. Heat gently, then taste for seasoning. Stir in plenty of parsley and serve at once, with parmesan cheese to sprinkle over the seafood and pasta.

COOK'S TIP

To clean squid, first wash it. Pull the head and tentacles from the body sac. Cut the tentacles off just above the head and slice them if you want to add them to the dish. Discard the other head parts and innards. Pull out the transparent quill which is inside the body sac, then rinse the sac well. Rub off the spotted skin to leave the squid clean and white. The flaps may rub off and these can be sliced separately. Slice the sac in thin rings.

Chicken and Tarragon Sauce

This is a simple sauce which goes well with any pasta. It may also be layered with lasagne, noodles or shapes in baked dishes. Turkey may be used instead of chicken.

SERVES 4

25–50 g/1–2 oz butter
1 small onion, finely chopped
1 bay leaf
100 g/4 oz button mushrooms, sliced
40 g/1½ oz plain flour
300 ml/½ pt chicken stock
150 ml/¼ pt milk
225–350 g/8–12 oz boneless, skinned, cooked chicken, diced
2 tbsp chopped tarragon
salt and freshly ground black pepper
150 ml/¼ pt single cream

Melt 25 g/1 oz butter in a saucepan. Add the onion and bay leaf and cook, stirring occasionally, for 15 minutes, or until the onion is softened slightly but not browned. Add the mushrooms and continue to cook for 10–15 minutes, until they give up their juice and this evaporates completely, leaving the reduced vegetables and the butter.

Stir in the flour, then gradually pour in the stock and bring to the boil, stirring all the time. Stir in the milk, bring back to the boil, then add the chicken and tarragon with seasoning to taste. Reduce the heat, cover the pan and simmer gently for 10 minutes. Stir in the cream and heat gently without boiling. If you like, beat in another 25 g/1 oz butter to enrich the sauce and make it rather special. Taste for seasoning before serving.

Duck and Orange Dressing

A rich dressing for narrow noodles or spaghetti, and a good way of making a couple of large duck breasts serve four. Make a salad of grated courgette and carrot as an accompaniment (see Cook's Tip).

SERVES 4

2 large boneless duck breasts, skinned and cut into fine strips

1 tbsp plain flour

salt and freshly ground black pepper

½ tsp ground mace

grated rind and juice of 1 orange

1 tbsp oil

1 onion, halved and thinly sliced

350 g/12 oz mushrooms, sliced

300 ml/½ pt dry red wine

4 tbsp redcurrant jelly

Place the duck meat in a bowl or polythene bag. Add the flour, plenty of seasoning, the mace and orange rind. Mix well, or close and shake the bag.

Heat the oil in a large frying pan. Add the duck and brown the strips all over, then add the onion and cook, stirring often, for about 15 minutes, or until the onion is softened slightly but not browned. Stir in the mushrooms and cook for 10 minutes or so, until they are well reduced. Pour in the orange juice and wine, then bring to the boil. Add the redcurrant jelly and boil for about 1 minute, stirring.

Taste for seasoning, then ladle the duck sauce over the pasta and serve at once.

COOK'S TIP

Carrot and Courgette Salad. Coarsely grate 3 carrots and 3 courgettes. Mix with a finely chopped spring onion and 4 shredded basil sprigs. Add 2 tbsp olive oil, a squeeze of orange juice and seasoning. Serve on a bed of iceberg lettuce.

Leek and Turkey Sauce

Boneless turkey breast fillets are versatile and in-expensive when combined with bulky vegetables and pasta. This is another sauce to serve with any pasta or to use in baked dishes and layer with lasagne.

SERVES 4

350 g/12 oz boneless turkey breast fillet, skinned and diced
4 tbsp plain flour
salt and freshly ground black pepper
2 tbsp oil
450 g/1 lb leeks, sliced
2 tbsp chopped sage
300 ml/½ pt dry cider
300 ml/½ pt turkey or chicken stock
2 tbsp freshly grated parmesan cheese
50 g/2 oz mozzarella cheese, chopped
150 ml/¼ pt Greek-style yogurt
a little paprika

Coat the turkey with the flour and plenty of season-ing. Heat the oil in a large saucepan. Add the turkey and cook, stirring often, until lightly browned. Add the leeks and sage, stir well, then cover the pan and cook for 15 minutes, stirring once or twice, until the leeks are greatly reduced in volume.

Stir in the cider and stock, then bring to the boil, stirring, and reduce the heat. Cover and simmer for 15 minutes, until the leeks are cooked. Stir in the parmesan and mozzarella, and taste for season-ing. When the cheeses have melted, stir in the yogurt and remove the pan from the heat. Serve at once, poured over pasta or tossed with it. Dust with a little paprika.

BELOW
Brilliantly coloured plants in the window of a house in Siena, Italy.

Chicken in Blue

Blue cheese makes a rich sauce for chicken or turkey. Serve large quantities of plain fresh pasta noodles to balance the full flavour of the sauce. I have used Danish blue but any other blue cheese may be substituted – dolcelatte, for example, or tangy gorgonzola for a really powerful flavour.

SERVES 4

2 tbsp olive oil
1 garlic clove, crushed
1 red pepper, seeded and diced
450 g/1 lb boneless chicken, skinned and diced
salt and freshly ground black pepper
225 g/8 oz small button mushrooms
4 tbsp dry white wine
150 ml/¼ pt single cream
225 g/8 oz Danish blue cheese, cut into small pieces
2 spring onions, finely chopped
2 tbsp chopped parsley

Heat the oil in a large frying pan. Add the garlic, red pepper and chicken with some seasoning – go easy on the salt at this stage as the blue cheese can make the sauce quite salty. Cook, stirring often, for about 20 minutes, or until the diced chicken is lightly browned and cooked.

Add the mushrooms and cook for 2 minutes, then pour in the wine and bring to the boil. Turn the heat to the lowest setting and make sure the mixture has stopped boiling before pouring in the cream and stirring in the cheese. Stir over low heat until the cheese has melted. Do not allow the sauce to simmer or it will curdle.

When the cheese has melted, taste the sauce, then pour it over the pasta and sprinkle with spring onions and parsley. Serve at once.

45

Steak Sauce with Salsa Aside

A really simple steak sauce, this one, with some onion and mushrooms to complement the flavour of the meat. The taste-bud awakener is the salsa aside – a Mexican-style cold sauce of tomato, onion and chilli. Serve it in a separate dish so that it can be spooned over the beef and pasta to taste. Noodles or spaghetti are the ideal pasta for this.

SERVES 4

225 g/8 oz ripe tomatoes, peeled (see Cook's Tip, page 26)
1 red onion, finely chopped
2 fresh green chillies, seeded and chopped
1 garlic clove, crushed
salt and freshly ground black pepper
1 tsp caster sugar

grated rind and juice of ½ lime
3 tbsp chopped coriander leaves
675 g/1½ lb lean rump steak, sliced across the grain and cut into strips (see Cook's Tip)
3 tbsp plain flour
large knob of beef dripping or 2 tbsp oil
1 large onion, halved and thinly sliced
1 bay leaf
2 parsley sprigs
2 thyme sprigs
350 g/12 oz mushrooms, sliced
450 ml/¾ pt good beef stock or canned consommé
dash of Worcestershire sauce

Make the salsa first but not too far in advance of serving. Halve the tomatoes, discard the cores leading from the stalks, then chop them. Mix with the onion, chillies and garlic. Add plenty of seasoning, the sugar, lime rind and juice, and the coriander. Mix well. Taste to check the seasoning and set aside.

Toss the steak with the flour and plenty of seasoning. Melt the dripping or heat the oil in a large frying pan. When the fat is shimmering hot add the steak and stir fry the strips until they are browned. If the fat is hot enough, and particularly if using dripping, the strips will seal, brown and cook quickly. Add the onion and herbs, reduce the heat and cook for 15 minutes, or until the onion is softened slightly. Stir in the mushrooms and cook for a further 15 minutes.

Pour in the stock and add Worcestershire sauce to taste. Bring to the boil, stirring, reduce the heat and simmer gently for 5 minutes. Taste for seasoning and remove the herb sprigs before serving.

COOK'S TIP

When cutting steak for frying as above, slice the meat across the grain, then cut the slices into strips. If the meat is cut with the grain the result is not as tender.

Rich Meat Ragout

This is a good Bolognese-style sauce for ladling over pasta or layering with it.

SERVES 4

3 tbsp olive oil
1 large onion, chopped
2 celery sticks, finely diced
2 carrots, finely diced
1 green pepper, seeded and diced
2 garlic cloves, crushed
100 g/4 oz rindless smoked bacon, diced
2 tsp dried marjoram
1 thyme sprig
1 bay leaf
225 g/8 oz lean minced pork
225 g/8 oz lean minced braising steak
salt and freshly ground black pepper
1 tbsp plain flour
1 tbsp tomato purée
2 × 400 g/14 oz cans chopped tomatoes
300 ml/½ pt dry red wine
4 tbsp chopped parsley
freshly grated parmesan cheese, to serve

Heat the oil in a large, heavy-based saucepan. Add the onion, celery, carrots, green pepper, garlic, bacon, marjoram, thyme and bay leaf. Cook, stirring, until the onion is slightly softened and the bacon cooked – about 15 minutes.

Add the pork and steak and continue to cook, stirring, for 10 minutes to mix and lightly cook the meats. Stir in plenty of seasoning, the flour and tomato purée. Stir in the tomatoes and wine, then bring the sauce to the boil. Reduce the heat, cover, and simmer the sauce for 1½ hours. Stir the sauce occasionally during cooking.

At the end of cooking, taste and adjust the seasoning before mixing in the parsley and serving the sauce ladled over pasta. Serve with parmesan cheese.

Pork with Dates and Ginger

Serve this sweet and slightly spicy dish with plain fine noodles or tagliatelle and a fresh onion salad (see Cook's Tip).

SERVES 4

2 tbsp oil

50 g/2 oz fresh root ginger, peeled and chopped

1 cinnamon stick

675 g/1½ lb lean boneless pork, diced

salt and freshly ground black pepper

100 g/4 oz fresh dates

150 ml/¼ pt fresh orange juice

150 ml/¼ pt water

150 ml/¼ pt soured cream

Heat the oil in a frying pan. Add the ginger, cinnamon and pork. Sprinkle in plenty of seasoning, then cook, stirring occasionally, until the pork is lightly browned and cooked through.

Meanwhile, slit the dates and remove their stones, then rub off their papery skins and slice the fruit. Add the orange juice and water to the pork. Bring to the boil, reduce the heat and simmer hard for 10 minutes. Stir in the dates, simmer for 5 minutes and taste for seasoning.

Remove the pan from the heat, swirl in the soured cream and serve at once, ladled over individual portions of pasta.

COOK'S TIP

Fresh Onion Salad. Thinly slice 2 red or white onions. Separate the slices into rings and place them in a bowl of iced water. Leave to soak for 30 minutes, or up to an hour. Drain well and pat dry on absorbent kitchen paper. Trim and roughly chop 1 bunch of watercress. Cut the tops from a tub of cress. Mix both types of cress and the onions. Sprinkle with salt, a little lemon juice and a little olive oil. Dust with paprika and serve.

Jalapeño Beef and Yam

Here's a recipe to transform old-fashioned stewed beef into a multi-national meal! Of course, a plain beef stew tastes really good with pasta but this is a bit different and the combination of yams and peppers makes the beef go a lot further.

SERVES 4

450 g/1 lb lean stewing beef, diced quite small
2 tbsp plain flour
salt and freshly ground black pepper
2 tbsp oil or knob of beef dripping
2 onions, chopped
600 ml/1 pt water
675 g/1½ lb yam, peeled and cut into 2.5 cm/1 in cubes
2 garlic cloves, crushed
1 red pepper, seeded and diced
1 green pepper, seeded and diced
100 g/4 oz can jalapeño chillies, drained and chopped
25 g/1 oz currants
grated rind and juice of 1 lime
2 tbsp chopped coriander leaves
2 tsp thyme leaves

Set the oven at 180°C/350°F/Gas 4. Coat the meat with flour and plenty of salt. Add a little pepper. Heat half the oil or dripping in a flameproof casserole. Add the meat and brown the pieces all over, then add half the chopped onion and cook for a few minutes. Pour in the water and bring to the boil. Cover the casserole tightly and transfer it to the oven. Cook for 1 hour, then reduce the heat to 160°C/325°F/Gas 3 and cook for a further 2 hours, or until the meat is very tender. Stir occasionally, scraping the side of the casserole to remove any residue which bakes on above the line of the stew.

Meanwhile, cook the yam in boiling water for 10 minutes, or until just tender. Drain. Heat the remaining oil or dripping and add the rest of the onion with the garlic, red and green peppers, chillies and currants. Cook over medium heat, stirring often, for 20 minutes, until the onion and peppers are well cooked. Stir in the lime rind and juice and herbs. Add the yam and mix well. Remove from the heat, cover and set aside until the beef is cooked. It is a good idea to prepare the yam mixture straight after the beef, so that the flavours have time to mingle and develop.

Stir the yam mixture into the stew and reheat thoroughly on the hob before serving. Ladle the sauce over bowls of tagliatelle or pasta shapes.

Sausage Meatball Sauce

SERVES 4

450 g/1 lb pork sausagemeat
1 onion, finely chopped
1 garlic clove, crushed
¼ tsp chilli powder
1 tsp ground coriander
salt and freshly ground black pepper
1 tsp dried oregano
1 tsp chopped thyme
1 tbsp chopped sage
75 g/3 oz fresh breadcrumbs
1 egg
1 tbsp oil
1 green pepper, seeded and diced
225 g/8 oz button mushrooms
½ quantity Good Tomato Sauce (page 56)

Place the sausagemeat in a bowl. Add the onion, garlic, chilli, coriander, seasoning, oregano, thyme, sage and breadcrumbs. Use a mixing spoon to break up the sausagemeat and mix in some of the other ingredients. When the sausagemeat is well broken up, add the egg. Then pound the ingredients together until thoroughly combined.

Wash your hands, then rinse them under cold water and keep them wet while you shape the meatballs to prevent the mixture sticking to them. Shape small, walnut-size meatballs.

Heat the oil in a large frying pan. Add the meatballs and brown them all over, using a spoon and fork to roll them around the pan. Add the green pepper and mushrooms and continue to cook for 10 minutes, or until the pepper is softened slightly. Pour in the tomato sauce and bring to the boil. Simmer for 20 minutes, turning the meatballs in the sauce occasionally. Serve piping hot.

Aubergine and Leek Topping

SERVES 4

2 large aubergines, trimmed and cubed

salt and freshly ground black pepper

4 tbsp olive oil

2 garlic cloves, crushed

¼ tsp chilli powder

450 g/1 lb leeks, sliced

2 tbsp tahini

450 ml/¾ pt stock (vegetable or chicken)

Place the aubergines in a colander and sprinkle them with salt, then leave them to stand over a bowl for 20 minutes. Rinse the aubergines well and leave to drain.

Heat half the olive oil in a large saucepan. Add some of the aubergine cubes and brown them on all sides. Use a slotted spoon to remove the cubes from the pan and set aside. Add more oil as necessary and cook the remaining cubes. Set aside. Add the garlic, chilli powder and leeks to the pan, then cook, stirring often, for 10 minutes, until the leeks are greatly reduced in volume.

Replace the aubergines and stir in the tahini, then pour in the stock and bring to the boil. Reduce the heat and cover the pan, then simmer for 15–20 minutes, until the aubergines and leeks are cooked through. Taste for seasoning before serving.

Broccoli and Baby Corn Dressing

SERVES 4

450 g/1 lb broccoli, cut into small florets

225 g/8 oz whole baby corn cobs

25 g/1 oz butter or 2 tbsp oil

1 onion, chopped

225 g/8 oz rindless bacon, diced

1 tbsp plain flour

salt and freshly ground black pepper

6 tbsp dry sherry

150 ml/¼ pt chicken or vegetable stock

freshly grated parmesan cheese, to serve

Place the broccoli in a steamer and cook over boiling water for 5 minutes. Add the baby corn cobs and cook for a further 5 minutes. Alternatively, cook the vegetables for the same time in the minimum of boiling water; they have a better flavour if they are steamed.

Melt the butter or heat the oil in a large saucepan. Add the onion and bacon, and cook, stirring often, until both are cooked. Stir in the flour and a little seasoning, then add the sherry and stock. Stir in the broccoli and corn. Bring to the boil, reduce the heat and cover the pan. Simmer for 5 minutes. Taste for seasoning.

Serve the vegetables and their sauce tossed into pasta. Offer parmesan cheese and extra ground pepper at the table.

Pumpkin Sauce

SERVES 4

3 tbsp olive oil

2 large onions, chopped

1 garlic clove, crushed

1 bay leaf

2 tbsp chopped sage

1 tsp dried marjoram

900 g/2 lb pumpkin, seeded, peeled and cubed

salt and freshly ground black pepper

100 g/4 oz mushrooms, sliced

2 × 400 g/14 oz cans chopped tomatoes

2 tbsp chopped parsley

freshly grated parmesan cheese, to serve

Heat the oil in a large saucepan. Add the onions, garlic, bay leaf, sage and marjoram. Cook, stirring, for 5 minutes, then add the pumpkin and mix well. Sprinkle in seasoning and continue to cook, stirring often, for 5 minutes. Stir in the mushrooms and tomatoes, heat until simmering and cover the pan. Cook gently for 35–40 minutes, until the pumpkin is tender but not mushy.

Stir in the parsley and taste for seasoning before serving, ladled over noodles or shapes. Offer parmesan cheese with the pumpkin sauce and pasta.

Pepper Sauce

SERVES 4–6

4 tbsp olive oil

2 garlic cloves, finely chopped

225 g/8 oz rindless bacon rashers, diced

1 onion, halved and thinly sliced

*2 red peppers, seeded, quartered lengthways
and cut in strips*

*2 green peppers, seeded, quartered lengthways
and cut in strips*

50 g/2 oz pine kernels

6 tbsp raisins

salt and freshly ground black pepper

150 ml/¼ pt dry sherry

Heat the oil in a large frying pan. Add the garlic, bacon, onion and red and green peppers. Cook, stirring often, for 5 minutes. Stir in the pine kernels and raisins with plenty of seasoning, then continue to cook, stirring occasionally, for 15 minutes.

Pour in the sherry and bring to the boil. Boil for 3 minutes. Taste and adjust the seasoning before pouring the sauce over the pasta. Toss well and serve at once.

Wonderful Mushroom Sauce

Look out for dried mushrooms in Italian and Eastern European delicatessens. This rich sauce, combining dried and fresh mushrooms, is delicious with plain noodles.

SERVES 4

2 whole dried mushrooms
150 ml/¼ pt boiling water
25 g/1 oz butter
1 tbsp olive oil
½ small onion, finely chopped
1 bay leaf
350 g/12 oz button mushrooms, sliced
100 ml/ 4 fl oz dry sherry
salt and freshly ground black pepper
350 g/12 oz oyster mushrooms
300 ml/½ pt single cream
3 tbsp chopped parsley
1 tbsp lemon juice

Place the dried mushrooms in a small basin and add the boiling water. Put a saucer on the mushrooms to keep them submerged and leave to soak for 15 minutes. Turn the mushrooms and the liquid into a small saucepan and simmer for 10 minutes, adding a little extra water if necessary. Drain, reserving the cooking liquor. Chop the mushrooms. Strain the liquor through a muslin-lined sieve or fine tea strainer to remove any grit.

Heat the butter and oil in a frying pan. Add the onion and bay leaf, then cook, stirring, for 5 minutes. Add the sliced mushrooms and continue to cook for 15–20 minutes. The mushrooms will give up their liquor and shrink: this stage is complete when all the liquid has evaporated, leaving the darkened mushrooms in the oil and butter, and it is important for a good flavour. Add the dried mushrooms and the strained liquid. Stir in the sherry and seasoning, then simmer for 5 minutes.

Add the oyster mushrooms and poach them in the sauce for 3 minutes, so that they are hot and lightly cooked. Stir in the cream, parsley and lemon juice. Heat gently without boiling. Taste for seasoning and serve ladled over fresh noodles.

Good Tomato Sauce

Good fresh pasta and a rich tomato sauce, topped with some freshly grated parmesan cheese, is a simple yet splendid meal, particularly if there is a really fresh, crisp green salad as an accompaniment. This sauce also has many uses in baked dishes or with stuffed pasta.

MAKES ABOUT 900 ML/1½ PT
SERVES 4–6

2 tbsp olive oil
1 large onion, chopped
1 carrot, chopped
1 celery stick, chopped
1 garlic clove, crushed
1 bay leaf
2 thyme sprigs
4 parsley sprigs
1 tbsp plain flour
2 tbsp tomato purée
900 g/2 lb ripe tomatoes, roughly chopped
1 tbsp sugar
150 ml/¼ pt dry red wine
salt and freshly ground black pepper
freshly grated parmesan cheese, to serve

Heat the oil in a large, heavy-based saucepan. Add the onion, carrot, celery, garlic, bay leaf, thyme and parsley. Cook, stirring, for 10 minutes, until the onion is softened slightly but not browned.

Stir in the flour and tomato purée. Then add the tomatoes and sugar and stir in the wine. Add some seasoning, bring to the boil and give the sauce a good stir. Reduce the heat, cover the pan and leave to simmer for 1 hour.

Remove the bay leaf and herb sprigs, then purée the sauce in a liquidizer and rub it through a sieve to remove the seeds. Reheat and taste for seasoning before serving. Ladle the sauce over pasta and top with parmesan cheese to taste.

Pesto

This is a wonderfully aromatic sauce based on basil. Grow a large pot of basil especially for the purpose of making pesto, or buy several cartons of the growing herb (if you plant the roots and shoots from the base of such cartons they will grow into large, healthy plants). Although pesto is traditionally made by pounding all the ingredients using a pestle and mortar, a food processor or liquidizer is more or less essential for the busy cook. If you do not have either, then work in far smaller quantities than those given below.

MAKES ABOUT 600 ML/1 PT

175 g/6 oz fresh parmesan cheese, rind removed
100 g/4 oz pine kernels
4 garlic cloves
50 g/2 oz basil sprigs (soft stems and leaves only, discard tough stalks before weighing)
350–450 ml/12–15 fl oz good-quality virgin olive oil
salt and freshly ground black pepper

Break the parmesan into small pieces and place in the food processor with the pine kernels and garlic. Process the mixture until the parmesan is finely crumbled. Add the basil and continue processing until the herb is chopped and the mixture begins to clump together into a coarse, bright green paste.

Add a little of the olive oil and process the mixture until it is incorporated, then gradually trickle in the remaining olive oil. Add enough to make a thin, pouring paste. Add seasoning to taste.

If using a liquidizer, process the mixture in batches. The oil does not form a mayonnaise-like liaison: it will separate on standing and the paste has to be stirred again. Mix all the batches together at the end so that the ingredients are combined in the correct proportions.

Transfer the pesto to a clean screw-top jar and store it in the refrigerator. The oil acts as a preservative and the pesto will keep for several months if stored in an airtight container in the refrigerator. Stir it well before using.

Top individual portions of pasta with a couple of spoons of pesto, then toss together and eat at once – delicious!

COOK'S TIP

If you are making a large batch of pesto for storing, sterilize the jars and their lids in a proprietary brand of sterilizing solution (from chemists; used for babies' bottles or for home brewing), then rinse them with boiling water and allow to dry by draining. Leave the jars upside down until you fill them with pesto.

LEFT
Tomatoes and grapes on a courtyard table . . . wonderful ingredients for fresh pasta recipes.

Béchamel Sauce

Well-cooked, good-quality pasta makes a delicious meal with the minimum of additions: in the Italian kitchen that means olive oil and garlic or butter with parmesan; to the traditional British cook a good milk-based sauce is ideal. Béchamel is a basic milk sauce which is lightly flavoured with bay and mace: it is used in a variety of pasta dishes, notably as the topping for baked lasagne.

MAKES ABOUT 600 ML/1 PT

1 thick onion slice
1 bay leaf
1 mace blade
2 parsley sprigs
600 ml/1 pt milk
40 g/1½ oz butter
40 g/1½ oz plain flour
salt and freshly ground white or black pepper

Place the onion, bay leaf, mace and parsley in a saucepan. Add the milk and heat slowly until just boiling. Remove from the heat, cover and leave for 45 minutes.

Strain the milk into a jug or basin. Wash the saucepan, then melt the butter and stir in the flour. Slowly pour in the milk, stirring all the time. Continue stirring until the sauce boils, then reduce the heat, if necessary, so that it just simmers. Cook for 3 minutes, stirring occasionally. Add seasoning to taste.

If the sauce is not used straight away, lay a piece of dampened greaseproof paper directly on its surface to prevent a skin forming.

Variations

Any one of the following may be mixed with freshly cooked pasta and served as a light meal. A gratin topping may be added by sprinkling the sauced pasta with 25 g/1 oz fresh breadcrumbs mixed with 2 tbsp freshly grated parmesan cheese and browning under the grill.

Cheese Sauce Stir in 100 g/4 oz grated mature Cheddar cheese and 4 tbsp freshly grated parmesan cheese after the sauce has simmered.

Egg Sauce Hard-boil and roughly chop 6 eggs, then mix them into the cooked sauce. Add 1 tbsp chopped tarragon or parsley, or 2 tbsp chopped dill, if liked.

Mushroom Sauce Add 225 g/8 oz sliced button mushrooms before the final simmering.

Onion Sauce Finely chop 2 large onions. Cook them in the butter for about 20 minutes, stirring often, until they are softened. Do not allow the onions to brown but do make sure that they are well cooked, otherwise the sauce will be inferior. Stir in the flour and continue as above.

Tuna Sauce Drain a 200 g/7 oz can of tuna. Flake the fish and add it to the sauce before the final simmering. Add 2 tbsp chopped parsley and 1 tbsp capers, chopped.

Tuna may be added to mushroom sauce, or an onion sauce may be prepared, then both mushrooms and tuna added. The oil from the can may be used instead of butter; brine may be added to the sauce with milk.

White Wine Sauce

MAKES 600 ML/1 PT

50 g/2 oz butter

1 small onion, finely chopped

1 bay leaf

2 parsley sprigs with long stalks

50 g/2 oz button mushrooms, thinly sliced

40 g/1½ oz plain flour

300 ml/½ pt dry white wine

150 ml/¼ pt stock (chicken, vegetable or fish, depending on the dish)

salt and freshly ground white or black pepper

300 ml/½ pt single cream

Melt the butter in a saucepan. Add the onion, bay leaf and parsley, then cook, stirring often, for 15 minutes, until the onion is softened slightly but not browned. Stir in the mushrooms, then stir in the flour. Gradually stir in the white wine and stock, then bring to the boil. The sauce will be too thick at this stage. Cover the pan tightly and allow the sauce to cook very gently for 15 minutes.

Add seasoning and beat the sauce well. Remove the bay leaf and parsley sprigs. Stir in the cream and heat gently without boiling.

BELOW
Vines growing at Monte Reggiano, Italy.

CHAPTER FOUR

HOT CREATIONS
Timbales, Moulds and Bakes

*This is one of the chapters which points out the versatility
of pasta, particularly when the dough is home-made
and ready to roll to any shape or size required. The majority
of these recipes are excellent for preparing ahead, so
glance through these pages if you are looking for
an idea next time you are cooking for friends.*

*Although cooked pasta does not freeze well as a separate ingredient, prepared
layered dishes with sauce are terrific freezer candidates. If you are planning on*

*freezing any of the dishes, remember that the freezer life of
the finished dish is only as long as the shortest recommended time
for the ingredients included in it. If that sounds rather confusing,
a classic example is bacon which has a short freezer life and
does go rancid, spoiling the flavour of a dish or sauce.*

*Whether you are looking for a hearty hotpot or an elegant first course, I am
sure you will find something in the pages which follow.*

Seafood Darioles

SERVES 4

75 g/3 oz pasta dough (page 14), rolled out and cut into small squares

butter for greasing

150 ml/¼ pt Cheese Sauce (page 58)

100 g/4 oz plaice fillet, skinned and chopped

100 g/4 oz peeled cooked prawns, thawed if frozen, chopped

1 tbsp chopped parsley

2 tbsp snipped chives

salt and freshly ground black pepper

1 egg, beaten

2 hard-boiled eggs

150 ml/¼ pt mayonnaise

3 tbsp single cream

1 tbsp chopped dill

dill or parsley and chives, to garnish

Cook the pasta in boiling salted water for 3 minutes, then drain. Set the oven at 180°C/350°F/Gas 4. Butter 4 dariole moulds and line their bases with non-stick baking parchment. Stand the moulds on a baking tray.

Mix the pasta with the sauce. Add the fish, prawns, parsley, chives, seasoning and beaten egg. Stir the mixture to make sure the ingredients are well combined, then divide it between the moulds. Cover with non-stick baking parchment and bake for 30 minutes.

Meanwhile, finely chop the hard-boiled eggs and mix them with the mayonnaise. Add seasoning to taste, then stir in the cream and dill. Slide a fine knife blade around the inside of each mould, then invert them on individual plates. Remove the non-stick baking parchment and spoon a little of the egg sauce beside each mould; offer the rest of the sauce separately. Garnish with herbs and serve at once.

BELOW
Fishing boats from the Mediterranean Sea, which provides squid, sardines, swordfish and prawns among its catches.

Salmon and Pasta Timbales

SERVES 4

50 g/2 oz turmeric-flavoured pasta dough (page 15)	*50 g/2 oz ricotta cheese, sieved*
salt and freshly ground black pepper	*salt and freshly ground black pepper*
200 g/7 oz can salmon	*1 egg, separated*
50 g/2 oz fresh white breadcrumbs	**To Garnish**
1 tbsp finely chopped spring onion	*basil or parsley sprigs*
3 basil sprigs, finely shredded, or 1 tbsp chopped parsley	*halved lemon slices*

HOT CREATIONS: TIMBALES, MOULDS AND BAKES

Roll out the pasta very thinly. Take a ramekin dish and cut a paper pattern of the base or find a round cutter to fit. Grease and base-line the ramekins with non-stick baking parchment. Cut 12 circles of pasta, then cook them in boiling salted water for 3 minutes. Drain the circles and place a circle of pasta in the bottom of each ramekin. Lay the remaining pasta out on absorbent kitchen paper. Set the oven at 180°C/350°F/Gas 4.

Drain the salmon, remove any skin and bone, then mash it. Mix with the breadcrumbs, spring onion, basil or parsley and ricotta cheese. Add seasoning and beat in the egg yolk. Whisk the egg white until stiff, then fold it into the salmon mixture.

Divide the mixture roughly in half, then spoon one portion into the dishes, dividing it equally between them and spreading it neatly. Top each with a circle of pasta, then divide the remaining mixture between the dishes. Finally, top each with a circle of pasta. Stand on a baking tray, cover with foil and bake for 25–30 minutes, or until the salmon mixture is set. It will also have risen.

Allow to stand for 2 minutes, then slide a knife around the inside of each ramekin. Invert the timbales on individual plates. Remove the non-stick baking parchment. Serve garnished with basil or parsley and lemon.

Seafood Lasagne

This is one of my favourite pasta dishes.

SERVES 6

350 g/12 oz spinach-flavoured pasta dough (page 15) or fresh lasagne verdi
2 tbsp olive oil
25 g/1 oz butter
1 onion, finely chopped
1 bay leaf
40 g/1½ oz plain flour
300 ml/½ pt dry white wine
300 ml/½ pt fish stock
100 g/4 oz button mushrooms, sliced
salt and freshly ground black pepper
675 g/1½ lb white fish fillet, skinned and cut into chunks
225 g/8 oz peeled cooked prawns, thawed if frozen
450 g/1 lb mussels, cooked and shelled (page 40)
2 tbsp chopped parsley
1 quantity Béchamel Sauce (page 58)
50 g/2 oz Cheddar cheese, grated

Cut the rolled-out pasta into large squares (about 12.5 cm/5 in) or oblong sheets. Lower the pieces of pasta one at a time into a large saucepan of boiling salted water. Bring back to the boil and cook for 3 minutes. Drain and rinse under cold water. Lay the pasta on double-thick sheets of absorbent kitchen paper.

Set the oven at 180°C/350°F/Gas 4. Heat the oil and butter in a saucepan and add the onion and bay leaf. Cook for 10 minutes, until the onion is softened slightly, then stir in the flour. Slowly pour in the wine and stock and bring to the boil, stirring all the time. Add the mushrooms and seasoning, then simmer for 10 minutes. Remove from the heat before stirring in the fish, prawns, mussels and parsley. Layer this fish sauce and the lasagne in a large ovenproof dish, ending with a layer of lasagne. Pour the béchamel sauce evenly over the pasta, then sprinkle the cheese on top. Bake for 40–50 minutes, until golden brown and bubbling hot.

Chicken and Ham Lasagne

This is easy and delicious! Turkey may be used instead of chicken – a great way of using up the Christmas roast. Add any leftover stuffing to the sauce too.

SERVES 6–8

350 g/12 oz spinach-flavoured pasta dough (page 15) or fresh lasagne verdi

2 quantities Béchamel Sauce

225 g/8 oz skinned, boneless cooked chicken, diced

225 g/8 oz lean cooked ham, diced

100 g/4 oz button mushrooms, chopped

6 spring onions, chopped

2 tbsp chopped parsley

1 tbsp chopped sage

salt and freshly ground black pepper

75 g/3 oz Caerphilly, Lancashire or Wensleydale cheese, finely crumbled

paprika

25 g/1 oz fresh white breadcrumbs

Prepare and cook the lasagne as for Classic Lasagne al Forno (page 64). Butter a 30–38 × 20 cm/12–15 × 8 in ovenproof dish and set the oven at 180°C/350°F/Gas 4.

Set aside a third of the béchamel sauce. Mix the chicken, ham, mushrooms, spring onions, parsley and sage with the rest of the sauce. Taste for seasoning, then layer this sauce in the dish with the lasagne, ending with a layer of lasagne on top. Stir the cheese into the reserved sauce (it doesn't matter if the sauce is too cool for it to melt), then spread it over the top of the pasta. Sprinkle with a little paprika and top with the breadcrumbs.

Bake for 40–50 minutes, until the topping is crisp and golden and the lasagne layers are bubbling hot.

COOK'S TIP

A mixture of crushed crisps and a few finely chopped salted peanuts added to the bread-crumbs makes a good topping.

RIGHT
Chicken and Ham Lasagne.

Classic Lasagne Al Forno

SERVES 6–8

350 g/12 oz pasta dough (page 14) or fresh lasagne

salt and freshly ground black pepper

butter for greasing

1 quantity Rich Meat Ragout (page 47)

1½ quantities Béchamel Sauce (page 58)

25 g/1 oz freshly grated parmesan cheese

Cut the rolled-out pasta into large squares (about 12.5 cm/5 in) or oblong sheets. Lower the pieces of pasta one at a time into a large saucepan of boiling salted water. Bring back to the boil and cook for 3 minutes. Drain and rinse under cold water. Lay the pasta on double-thick sheets of absorbent kitchen paper.

Set the oven at 180°C/350°F/Gas 4. Butter a large oblong ovenproof dish (about 30–38 × 20 cm/12–15 × 8 in). Ladle a little of the ragout into the dish and spread it out. Dot with a little of the béchamel sauce, then add a layer of pasta. Continue layering the meat, a little béchamel and pasta, ending with pasta. Do not include much béchamel between the layers as you need most of it to cover the top of the lasagne. Sprinkle the parmesan over the top and bake the lasagne for 45–50 minutes, until golden brown and bubbling hot.

Tagliatelle Turkey Bake

SERVES 4–6

2 tbsp olive oil

1 onion, chopped

1 garlic clove, crushed

1 green pepper, seeded and diced

1 tsp dried marjoram

350 g/12 oz skinned, boneless cooked turkey, diced

100 g/4 oz mushrooms, thinly sliced

400 g/14 oz can chopped tomatoes

3 tbsp chopped parsley

salt and freshly ground black pepper

450 g/1 lb tagliatelle, cooked

4 fresh basil sprigs

600 ml/1 pint Béchamel Sauce (page 58)

100 g/4 oz mozzarella cheese, diced

2 tbsp freshly grated parmesan cheese

Set the oven at 200°C/400°F/Gas 6. Heat the oil in a large saucepan. Add the onion, garlic, green pepper and marjoram. Cook, stirring often, for 15–20 minutes, until the onion is softened. Stir in the turkey, mushrooms, tomatoes, parsley and seasoning. Remove from the heat and mix in the tagliatelle. Turn the mixture into an ovenproof dish and press the top down with the back of a metal spoon so the noodles are fairly flat.

Use scissors to shred the basil and soft stalks into the béchamel sauce. Taste for seasoning, then pour the sauce evenly over the pasta mixture. Mix the mozzarella and parmesan, then sprinkle this over the sauce. Bake for 40–45 minutes, until the topping is browned.

Asparagus Roulades

Halve the quantities if you want to serve these as a light first course.

SERVES 4

½ quantity pasta dough (page 14)
butter for greasing
100 g/4 oz cream cheese
4 tbsp freshly grated parmesan cheese
2 tbsp snipped chives
25 g/1 oz fresh breadcrumbs
salt and freshly ground black pepper
32 fine asparagus spears, lightly cooked (page 24)
1 quantity Béchamel Sauce (page 58)

Roll out the pasta into a long sheet, slightly larger than 25 × 50 cm/10 × 20 in. (If it is more practical, roll out the dough in two batches.) Trim the dough neatly, cut it in half lengthways, then across at 8 equal intervals. This will make 16 oblongs measuring 12.5 × 6 cm/5 × 2½ in. Cook these in boiling salted water for 3 minutes, drain, rinse in cold water and lay out on double-thick absorbent kitchen paper.

Set the oven at 200°C/400°F/Gas 6. Butter an ovenproof dish. Mix the cream cheese, half the parmesan, the chives and breadcrumbs. Add a little seasoning. Spread or dot a little of the cheese mixture over a piece of pasta, then lay a couple of asparagus spears on top and roll the pasta over to enclose them. Lay in the dish with the join in the pasta down. Fill all the pasta in the same way.

Pour the béchamel sauce over the pasta and sprinkle with the remaining parmesan. Bake for 20–25 minutes, until bubbling hot and lightly browned on top.

Spiced Marrow and Pasta Bake

This is also a good recipe for pumpkin. Buy only good-quality curry powder prepared by a reputable manufacturer as the cheaper anonymous types can be revolting.

SERVES 4

25 g/1 oz butter	225 g/8 oz mushrooms, sliced
1 onion, chopped	25 g/1 oz ground almonds
1 garlic clove, crushed	1 tbsp plain flour
675 g/1½ lb marrow, seeded, peeled and cut in small cubes	300 ml/½ pt coconut milk (see Cook's Tip)
1 tsp mild curry powder	grated rind of 1 lime
	salt and freshly ground black pepper
	350 g/12 oz pasta spirals, cooked
	300 ml/½ pt single cream
	25 g/1 oz flaked almonds

Set the oven at 180°C/350°F/Gas 4. Melt the butter in a large saucepan. Add the onion and garlic and cook for 5 minutes, then stir in the marrow, curry powder and mushrooms. Cook for 25–30 minutes, stirring often, until the marrow is tender. Stir in the ground almonds and flour, then pour in the coconut milk, stirring all the time, and bring to simmering point. Remove from the heat and add the lime rind with seasoning to taste.

Mix the pasta with the cream and turn half of it into an ovenproof dish or casserole. Spread the pasta out in an even layer, then top with the marrow mixture, then cover with the remaining pasta in an even layer. Sprinkle the almonds over the top and bake for 30 minutes, until lightly browned on top.

COOK'S TIP

Coconut milk can be made as follows: soak desiccated or freshly grated coconut in boiling water, and cover for 30 minutes. Then squeeze out all the liquid, pressing the mixture with a spoon in a sieve. Alternatively, you can buy instant coconut milk powder and dilute it according to the packet instructions.

Cauliflower and Stilton Terrine

SERVES 6

450 g/1 lb cauliflower
175 g/6 oz blue stilton cheese, finely crumbled
100 g/4 oz fresh white breadcrumbs
8 spring onions, finely chopped
1 tbsp chopped sage
150 ml/¼ pt soured cream
4 tbsp dry sherry
2 eggs
salt and freshly ground black pepper
freshly grated nutmeg
butter for greasing
½ quantity spinach-flavoured pasta dough (page 15) or fresh lasagne verdi
Good Tomato Sauce (page 56) to serve

Cook the cauliflower in boiling water for 5 minutes, then drain well before chopping the florets. Mix the cauliflower, stilton, breadcrumbs, spring onions, sage, soured cream, sherry and eggs. Add seasoning and a little nutmeg.

Set the oven at 180°C/350°F/Gas 4. Prepare a bain marie and butter a 900 g/2 lb loaf tin. Cut the fresh pasta into wide strips which are long enough to line the tin widthways and overhang the sides. Cook the pasta for 3 minutes, drain and rinse in cold water, then lay out to dry on double-thick absorbent kitchen paper.

Line the tin completely with bands of pasta, overlapping them neatly. If bought fresh lasagne is not long enough, then overlap strips as you do need some pasta overhanging the rim of the tin. Spread a layer of cauliflower mixture in the base of the tin, then cover with a layer of pasta, cutting it to fit neatly and overlapping pieces as necessary. Continue layering cauliflower mixture and pasta until the tin is full, ending with cauliflower mixture.

Fold the ends of the pasta over. Add a final layer of pasta to cover the top of the terrine neatly. Generously butter a piece of greaseproof paper and lay it on top of the pasta. Cover with foil, sealing it well around the edges of the tin. Stand the tin in the bain marie and bake it for 1½ hours, until the mixture is firm to the touch and cooked through. Allow to stand for 5 minutes after cooking.

Slide a palette knife between the pasta and the tin, then invert the terrine on a flat platter. Use a serrated knife to cut the terrine into thick slices and serve with tomato sauce.

Pork and Pasta Rolls

SERVES 4

450 g/1 lb minced pork

50 g/2 oz fresh white breadcrumbs

1 onion, finely chopped

1 tbsp chopped rosemary

2 tbsp chopped parsley

2 eggs, beaten

salt and freshly ground black pepper

1/2 quantity carrot-flavoured pasta dough (page 15)

300 ml/1/2 pt dry cider

600 ml/1 pt chicken stock

40 g/1 1/2 oz butter

15 g/1/2 oz plain flour

rosemary sprigs to garnish (optional)

Mix the pork, breadcrumbs, onion, rosemary, parsley and half the beaten egg. Add plenty of seasoning and pound the mixture until all the ingredients are thoroughly combined.

Roll out the dough into an oblong measuring slightly larger than 42 × 25 cm/17 × 10 inches. Trim the edges, then brush the pasta with beaten egg. Spread the meat mixture all over the roll, leaving a narrow border around the edge. Roll up the pasta from the long end. Seal the end of the roll with more beaten egg and press it down on the roll with a blunt knife.

Set the oven at 180°C/350°F/Gas 4. Prepare a large saucepan of boiling water. Cut the roll in half or quarters, depending on the size of the saucepan. Carefully lower the pieces of roll into the water and simmer for 3 minutes. Wrapping a couple of bands of folded foil around the roll helps with lowering it into the water and lifting it out again; otherwise use a large fish slice and slotted spoon to drain the pieces of roll. Cut the roll into 16 slices and place them in an ovenproof casserole.

Heat the cider and stock together, then pour them over the rolls, cover and bake for 1 hour. Meanwhile, beat the butter into the flour. Transfer the cooked rolls to a serving dish or individual plates and keep hot. Bring the cooking juices to the boil in a saucepan, then gradually whisk in the butter and flour paste. Boil for 3 minutes, then taste for seasoning. Spoon a little of the sauce over the rolls and offer the rest separately. Garnish with fresh rosemary sprigs if you like.

RIGHT
One of the most famous views in Italy – the Brunelleschi dome of Florence Cathedral.

Turkey and Lasagne Ring

SERVES 4

100 g/4 oz spinach-flavoured pasta dough (page 15) or fresh lasagne verdi
100 g/4 oz pasta dough (page 14) or fresh lasagne
2 tbsp oil
450 g/1 lb leeks, chopped
450 g/1 lb boneless turkey, skinned and diced
1 cooking apple, peeled, cored and chopped
50 g/2 oz fresh breadcrumbs
2 tbsp chopped sage
salt and freshly ground black pepper
1 egg
Mushroom Sauce (page 58) to serve

Roll out both doughs separately and cut them into wide bands, or lasagne, long enough to line a ring tin. Cook the lasagne in boiling salted water for 3 minutes, then drain and rinse it under cold water. Lay out on double-thick absorbent kitchen paper.

Heat the oil in a large saucepan. Add the leeks and cook for about 15 minutes, until they are greatly reduced in volume and softened. Remove from the heat. Mix in the turkey, apple, breadcrumbs, sage, plenty of seasoning and egg. Make sure the ingredients are thoroughly combined.

Set the oven at 180°C/350°F/Gas 4. Grease a 1.1 litre/2 pt ring tin. Line it with lasagne, alternating the verdi and plain sheets, and leaving the pasta overlapping the rim of the tin. Fill with the turkey mixture, then fold the ends of the lasagne over neatly. Cover with greased foil and bake for 1 hour. Check that the turkey mixture is cooked through by inserting the point of a knife into the middle of it and taking out a small portion.

Invert the ring on a platter. Cut into slices to serve and offer mushroom sauce to pour over individual portions.

COOK'S TIP

Fill the middle of the ring with vegetables, such as sautéed courgettes, glazed carrots or French beans sautéed with red peppers and onions.

Lamb and Pasta Hotpot

This is a heart-warming winter stew! Beef, pork or bacon may all be used instead of lamb. Offer some crusty bread to mop up the juices.

SERVES 4

1 tbsp oil

550 g/1¼ lb lean boneless lamb, cubed

1 onion, chopped

2 carrots, diced

2 rosemary sprigs

salt and freshly ground black pepper

600 ml/1 pt light ale

600 ml/1 pt water

225 g/8 oz frozen peas

450 g/1 lb pasta spirals

150 ml/¼ pt soured cream

paprika

croûtons, to serve

Heat the oil in a large flameproof casserole or heavy-based saucepan. Add the lamb and brown the cubes all over. Stir in the onion, carrots, rosemary sprigs and seasoning. Cook, stirring, for a few minutes, then add the ale and water. Bring just to the boil, reduce the heat and cover the pan. Leave the hotpot to simmer for 1¼ hours, stirring occasionally until the lamb is tender and the cooking liquor is well flavoured.

Taste for seasoning, then add the peas. Bring back to the boil, reduce the heat and cover the pot. Simmer for 15 minutes. Add the pasta, stir well, then bring back to the boil. Partially cover the pan and cook for 5 minutes, allowing the hotpot to only just boil.

Top individual portions of the hotpot with soured cream and sprinkle with paprika. Sprinkle with croûtons and serve piping hot.

Venison on a Bed of Pasta

Venison is delicious in this lightly spiced, creamy sauce. For a cheaper alternative, prepare a braising joint of beef, such as chuck, in the same way. Ask the butcher to truss the joint neatly so that it stays in good shape during cooking. Serve with French beans and glazed carrot strips.

SERVES 6

1.4 kg/3 lb boneless joint of leg of venison
1 onion, thinly sliced
1 carrot, diced
1 tbsp coriander seeds, coarsely crushed
1 tsp green peppercorns, crushed
1 bay leaf
1 bottle dry white wine
2 tbsp pistachio oil
2 tbsp oil
100 g/4 oz rindless bacon, diced
salt and freshly ground black pepper
100 g/4 oz stoned prunes, roughly chopped
100 g/4 oz chestnut mushrooms, sliced
40 g/1½ oz butter
25 g/1 oz plain flour
450 g/1 lb noodles
300 ml/½ pt soured cream

Place the venison in a mixing bowl. Add the onion, carrot, coriander seeds, peppercorns and bay leaf. Pour the wine over the meat, then trickle the pistachio oil over. Cover and leave to marinate in the refrigerator for 24 hours, turning the meat in the marinade as often as possible.

Heat the oil in a large flameproof casserole or heavy-based saucepan. Brown the joint of venison very well on all sides. Add the bacon, cook for 2–3 minutes, then add all the marinade. Add plenty of seasoning and pour in enough water to two-thirds cover the venison. Bring just to the boil, reduce the heat and cover with a close-fitting lid. Simmer for 1½ hours, then carefully turn the joint. Add the prunes and mushrooms and cook for a further 1¼ hours. Cream the butter and flour to a smooth paste and set aside.

Add the noodles to the pan. Bring back to the boil, then reduce the heat and simmer for a further 10 minutes. Lift the venison from the pan. Use a slotted spoon to transfer the noodles to a heated serving dish. Cover and keep hot. Boil the cooking liquid rapidly in the open pan until it is reduced to about 450 ml/¾ pt.

Meanwhile, carve the venison and arrange it on top of the noodles. Cover and keep hot. Whisk the flour paste into the sauce and boil for 2 minutes, whisking all the time. Remove from the heat, stir in the soured cream and taste for seasoning. Heat gently if necessary but do not boil. Pour some of the sauce over the meat and noodles and offer the rest separately.

CHAPTER FIVE

STUFFED PASTA
Filling For Flavour

Home-made stuffed pasta really is worth the effort for the quality is evident in the texture of the filling as well as in the flavours. Although it can take a while to get

started, once you have a "filling, shaping and sealing" production line going, and you have got the feel for your dough, it is surprising how relaxing stuffing pasta can be . . . rather like eating it, in fact.

Before you start to pile up the finished pasta shapes, prepare a large platter or roasting tin for holding them by dusting it with flour. Keep the finished pasta lightly dusted with flour if you have to pile it up, otherwise the shapes will stick together and break.

If the dough dries out as you are filling cut pieces it will be difficult to handle and seal, so keep it loosely covered with cling

film or polythene. Do not be over-ambitious about the quantity of filling which will fit into small pieces of pasta. Most of the fillings are well seasoned, so a little gives a lot of flavour whereas too much will only split the dough casing during cooking. Brush the dough edges with a little egg but do not make them too wet: not only does this make filling the dough a messy task, it also causes the two edges to slip apart. Lastly, remember that the cooking time for stuffed pasta shapes such as ravioli depends on the type of filling — raw meat filling takes longer to cook through than a cooked mixture does.

Tuna Triangles

SERVES 6–8

200 g/7 oz can tuna, drained

2 tbsp finely chopped spring onion

1 garlic clove, crushed

50 g/2 oz fresh white breadcrumbs

grated rind of ½ lemon

4 tbsp freshly grated parmesan cheese

salt and freshly ground black pepper

about 3 tbsp milk

⅔ quantity pasta dough (page 14)

1 egg, beaten

Good Tomato Sauce (page 56),
White Wine Sauce (page 59),
Cheese Sauce (page 58) or Mushroom Sauce (page 58)

freshly grated parmesan cheese, to serve

Mash the tuna, then mix in the spring onion, garlic and breadcrumbs. Add the lemon rind, parmesan cheese and seasoning to taste. Mix in just enough milk to bind the mixture.

Roll out half the pasta dough into a 32 cm/12½ in square. Cut it into 5 × 6 cm/2½ in strips, then cut these across into squares. Brush a square of dough with a little egg. Place a little tuna mixture on the middle of the dough, then fold it in half in a triangular shape. Pinch the edges together well to seal in the filling. Repeat with the remainder of the rolled dough, then do the same with the second half.

Bring a large saucepan of salted water to the boil. Add the triangles and bring the water back to the boil. Do not let the water boil too rapidly or the pasta may burst: keep it just boiling steadily. Cook for 4–5 minutes, then drain well.

Serve the triangles with any one of the sauces listed and offer parmesan cheese at the table.

Savoury Sardine Cannelloni

An inexpensive dish for a mid-week meal. The sardine and cheese mixture is also good for filling ravioli or tortellini.

SERVES 4

¹/₃ quantity pasta dough (page 14)

2 × 120 g/4 oz cans sardines in oil

1 onion, chopped

1 garlic clove, crushed

75 g/3 oz fresh white breadcrumbs

100 g/4 oz mushrooms, chopped

100 g/4 oz curd cheese

100 g/4 oz Cheddar cheese, grated

grated rind and juice of 1 lemon

salt and freshly ground black pepper

butter for greasing

1 quantity Good Tomato Sauce (page 56)

Roll out the pasta into a thin 40 cm/16 in square. Cut it into 4 × 10 cm/4 in wide strips, then cut the strips across to make 16 squares. Bring a large pan of salted water to the boil and cook the pieces of pasta, a few at a time if necessary, for 3 minutes. Drain and rinse under cold water, then lay out on double-thick absorbent kitchen paper.

Pour the oil from the sardines into a small saucepan. Add the onion and garlic, then cook, stirring often, for 10 minutes. Remove from the heat. Mash the sardines and add them to the onion and garlic. Mix in the breadcrumbs, mushrooms, curd cheese, three-quarters of the Cheddar cheese, the lemon rind and juice, and seasoning to taste.

Set the oven at 200°C/400°F/Gas 6. Butter an ovenproof dish. Place some of the sardine mixture on a piece of pasta, then roll it up into a neat tube and place in the dish with the end of the roll underneath. Repeat with the remaining pasta and filling. Ladle the tomato sauce over the cannelloni, then sprinkle with the remaining cheese. Bake for 25–30 minutes, until the cheese has melted and browned. Serve at once.

Chicken Tortellini

225 g/8 oz skinned, boneless cooked chicken, minced
25 g/1 oz fresh white breadcrumbs
2 tbsp very finely chopped onion
1 tbsp chopped sage
2 tbsp chopped parsley
4 tbsp single cream or milk
salt and freshly ground black pepper
⅔ quantity pasta dough (page 14)
1 egg, beaten
White Wine Sauce (page 59) or Good Tomato Sauce (page 56)
freshly grated parmesan cheese, to serve

Mix the chicken, breadcrumbs, onion, sage, parsley and cream or milk. Add seasoning and pound the mixture with the spoon to ensure all the ingredients are thoroughly combined.

Cut the pasta dough in half. Roll out one piece into a 30 cm/12 in square – it is a good idea to roll the dough nominally larger, then trim it neatly. Cut the dough into 6 × 5 cm/2 in strips, then cut across these to make 5 cm/2 in squares. Brush a square of dough with a little egg, then place a little of the chicken filling in the middle of it. Seal two opposite corners together to make a triangular shape. Wrap the long side of the triangle around your fingertip and pinch the corners together to make a mitre shape (or bishop's hat shape). Continue filling and sealing the tortellini, then roll out the second portion of dough and repeat the process. Do not overfill the tortellini or they will burst during cooking.

Bring a large saucepan of salted water to the boil. Add the tortellini and bring the water back to the boil. Do not boil the pasta too rapidly or they will split. Cook for 5 minutes, then drain well. Serve the tortellini with White Wine Sauce or Good Tomato Sauce and offer parmesan cheese at the table.

Alternative Serving Ideas
▌ Toss the tortellini in hot melted butter and parmesan cheese.
▌ Serve with Béchamel Sauce (page 58).
▌ Serve with Pesto (page 57).
▌ Serve the tortellini in soup, such as consommé or chicken broth.

Pork and Rosemary Ravioli

Depending on where you are in Italy, ravioli may be square or round. Round filled pasta may also be referred to as agnolotti, again according to regional preferences and traditions.

SERVES 12

2 tbsp olive oil

1 onion, finely chopped

2 garlic cloves, crushed

4 juniper berries, crushed

1 tbsp chopped rosemary

½ tsp ground mace

350 g/12 oz lean minced pork

50 g/2 oz fresh white breadcrumbs

50 g/2 oz mushrooms, chopped

salt and freshly ground black pepper

2 eggs

1 quantity pasta dough (page 14)

To serve

White Wine Sauce (page 59)

100 g/4 oz button mushrooms, thinly sliced

2 tbsp chopped parsley

freshly grated parmesan cheese

Heat the oil in a saucepan. Add the onion, garlic and juniper berries. Cook, stirring, for 15 minutes, or until the onion is softened. Stir in the rosemary, mace, pork, breadcrumbs, mushrooms and plenty of seasoning. Add 1 egg and thoroughly mix the ingredients, pounding them with the back of the spoon. Beat the remaining egg.

Roll out half the pasta dough slightly larger than a 45 cm/18 in square. Use a 5 cm/2 in round cutter to stamp out circles of pasta, dipping the cutter in flour occasionally so that it cuts the dough cleanly. The best way to do this is to stamp all the circles close together in neat lines in the dough, then lift away the unwanted trimmings when the whole sheet is stamped into circles. You should have about 80 circles. Keep the circles which are not actually being used covered with cling film while you fill the ravioli. Brush a circle of dough with egg, then place some of the meat mixture on it and cover with a second circle of dough. Pinch the edges of the dough together to seal in the filling. Fill all the ravioli, then roll out the remaining dough and make a second batch.

Cook the ravioli in a large saucepan of boiling water, allowing 15 minutes once the water has come back to the boil. Do this in batches if necessary, then drain the pasta.

Make the sauce but do not add the cream. Add the mushrooms and simmer for 5 minutes before stirring in the cream and parsley. Pour the sauce over the ravioli and serve with parmesan cheese.

Beef Ravioli with Tomato Sauce

SERVES 6

1 tbsp oil
½ onion, finely chopped
1 garlic clove, crushed
½ tsp dried marjoram
¼ tsp chopped thyme
¼ tsp ground coriander
salt and freshly ground black pepper
100 g/4 oz rump steak, finely minced
50 g/2 oz lean bacon, minced
25 g/1 oz fresh white breadcrumbs
1 egg, beaten
⅔ quantity pasta dough (page 14)
1 quantity Good Tomato Sauce (page 56)
freshly grated parmesan cheese, to serve

Heat the oil in a small saucepan. Add the onion, garlic, marjoram, thyme, coriander and seasoning. Cook, stirring, for 5 minutes, then remove from the heat. Mix in the steak, bacon and breadcrumbs. Add a little of the egg to bind the ingredients. Pound the mixture until thoroughly mixed.

Cut the pasta dough in half. Roll out one half into an oblong measuring slightly larger than 35.5 × 25 cm/14 × 10 in. Trim the edges of the dough neatly. Cover the rolled out dough with cling film, then roll out the second portion of dough in the same way but do not bother to trim the edges this time, as a little more dough is needed to cover the stuffing.

Dot small balls of the meat mixture in even lines over the neat oblong of pasta dough, leaving a gap of about 2 cm/¾ in between them. You should have 34–36 ravioli. Whisk a little water into the remaining beaten egg, to make it go further if necessary, then brush it over the dough between the mounds of meat. Carefully lay the second sheet of dough over the top. Starting at one end, seal the dough around the meat, carefully pressing out the air and flattening the meat slightly to seal the packages. Use a sharp knife or pastry wheel to trim the pasta edges and cut between the mounds of meat. Make sure the ravioli are neat and flour them slightly, if necessary, to prevent them sticking together.

Bring a large saucepan of salted water to the boil. Reduce the heat slightly so that it is not bubbling too rapidly and add the ravioli. Keep the water just boiling steadily and cook the ravioli for 10–15 minutes. Meanwhile, heat the tomato sauce. Drain the ravioli, turn them into a serving dish and pour the tomato sauce over them. Mix lightly before serving with parmesan cheese.

Walnut Cheese Ravioli

SERVES 6

2 tbsp olive oil

1 small onion, finely chopped

1 garlic clove, crushed

100 g/4 oz walnuts, finely chopped

100 g/4 oz ricotta cheese

75 g/3 oz gruyère cheese

2 tbsp freshly grated parmesan cheese

6 basil sprigs, finely shredded

50 g/2 oz fresh white breadcrumbs

salt and freshly ground black pepper

⅔ quantity pasta dough (page 14)

1 egg, beaten

White Wine Sauce (page 59) or hot melted butter to serve

Heat the oil in a small saucepan. Add the onion and garlic and cook for 15 minutes, until the onion is softened but not browned. Remove from the heat, then stir in the walnuts, ricotta, gruyère, parmesan cheese, basil and breadcrumbs. Add seasoning to taste and mix the ingredients thoroughly.

Make the ravioli as for the Beef Ravioli with Tomato Sauce (page 79), making sure the mixture is well sealed in the packets. Cook the ravioli for 5 minutes in water which is just boiling, as the cheese filling does not take as long to cook through as the raw beef filling. Drain and serve with Wine Sauce or simply with butter and pepper.

Spinach and Ricotta Tortellini

SERVES 6–8

175 g/6 oz fresh spinach, trimmed and cooked

100 g/4 oz ricotta cheese

4 tbsp freshly grated parmesan cheese

25 g/1 oz fresh white breadcrumbs

pinch of dried thyme

1 tsp dried marjoram

a little freshly grated nutmeg

salt and freshly ground black pepper

⅔ quantity pasta dough (page 14)

1 egg, beaten

Make sure the spinach is thoroughly drained, then chop it finely. Mix it with the ricotta, parmesan, breadcrumbs and herbs. Add a little nutmeg and seasoning to taste.

Use the dough and beaten egg to make and fill the tortellini, following the instructions for Chicken Tortellini (page 77). Cook and serve the tortellini in the same way.

Harvest Moons

These are unusual, filling and nutritious – good if you like spiced food and ideal for a vegetarian lunch.

SERVES 4

1 tbsp oil
1/2 small onion, chopped
1/2 small carrot, chopped
1 garlic clove, crushed
1 tsp cumin seeds
1 tsp ground coriander

1/2 × 400 g/14 oz can chick peas, drained
1 tomato, peeled and chopped
2 tsp chopped coriander leaves
salt and freshly ground black pepper
1/2 quantity turmeric-flavoured pasta dough (page 15)
1 egg, beaten
50 g/2 oz lightly salted butter
1/2 cucumber, peeled and diced
2 tbsp chopped mint

Heat the oil in a small saucepan. Add the onion, carrot, garlic and cumin seeds. Cook, stirring often, for 10 minutes. Stir in the coriander and cook for 2 minutes, then remove the pan from the heat. Roughly mash the chick peas – they should not be completely smooth. Stir the chick peas into the onion mixture, then add the tomatoes, chopped coriander and seasoning to taste.

Roll the pasta dough into a 45 cm/18 in square. Use a 5 cm/2 in round cutter to stamp out circles of pasta, dipping the cutter in flour occasionally so that it cuts the dough cleanly. The best way to do this is to stamp all the circles close together in neat lines in the dough, then lift away the unwanted trimmings when the whole sheet is stamped into circles. You should have about 80 circles. Keep the circles which are not actually being used covered with cling film while you fill some of them.

Brush a circle of dough with egg, then place some of the chick pea mixture on it. Fold the pasta in half to make a tiny pasty shape. Pinch the edges of the dough together to seal in the filling. Repeat with the remaining pasta circles. Cook the moons in boiling salted water, allowing 3–5 minutes after the water comes back to the boil.

While the pasta is cooking, heat the butter. Add the cucumber and mint and set aside over low heat. Turn the cooked pasta into a warmed serving dish and pour the butter and cucumber mixture over. Toss well, then serve at once.

Three-Cheese Cannelloni

Only good-quality parmesan cheese is suitable for the filling in these cannelloni. Bought grated parmesan, which is strong but lacking the sweetness of a good cheese, will taste too pungent. A fresh, crisp and extremely simple green salad is the perfect accompaniment to complement the richness of the cheese and tomato in the baked dish.

SERVES 4

⅓ quantity pasta dough (page 14)
225 g/8 oz ricotta cheese
75 g/3 oz freshly grated parmesan cheese
100 g/4 oz fresh white breadcrumbs
1 tsp dried oregano
1 bunch watercress, trimmed and chopped
salt and freshly ground black pepper
freshly grated nutmeg
butter for greasing
1 quantity Good Tomato Sauce (page 56)
175 g/6 oz mozzarella cheese, thinly sliced
handful of basil sprigs

Roll out the pasta thinly into a 40 cm/16 in square. Cut it into 4 × 10 cm/4 in wide strips, then cut the strips across to make 16 squares. Bring a large pan of salted water to the boil and cook the pieces of pasta, a few at a time if necessary, for 3 minutes. Drain and rinse under cold water, then lay out on double-thick absorbent kitchen paper.

Mix the ricotta, parmesan, breadcrumbs, oregano and watercress. Add seasoning and a little grated nutmeg to taste, then stir the mixture to make sure all the ingredients are thoroughly combined.

Set the oven at 200°C/400°F/Gas 6. Butter an ovenproof dish. Place some of the cheese mixture on a piece of pasta, then roll it up into a neat tube and place in the dish with the end of the roll underneath. Repeat with the remaining pasta and filling. Ladle the tomato sauce over the cannelloni, then top with the mozzarella. Bake for 25–30 minutes, until the cheese has melted and browned. Use scissors to shred the basil leaves and soft stems and sprinkle it over the cannelloni. Serve at once.

Aubergine Parcels

Halve the quantities if you want to serve one parcel per person for a light main course or starter.

SERVES 4

2 small aubergines
salt and freshly ground black pepper
4–6 tbsp olive oil
2 large slices lean cooked ham
8 sage leaves
225 g/8 oz (8 small slices) dolcelatte cheese
²/₃ quantity pasta dough (page 14)
2 large onions, thinly sliced
450 g/1 lb ripe tomatoes, peeled and sliced
100 g/4 oz soft cheese with garlic and herbs
50 g/2 oz fine dry white breadcrumbs
4 tbsp freshly grated parmesan cheese

Trim the aubergines and cut eight slices. Layer these in a colander with a little salt, place over a bowl, then leave to stand for 30 minutes. Rinse well and dry on absorbent kitchen paper.

Heat some olive oil in a frying pan and brown the aubergines on both sides, adding more oil as necessary. Cut the ham into 8 pieces. Sandwich the aubergine slices in pairs, placing a piece of ham, sage leaf and slice of dolcelatte between each pair.

Roll out half the dough into a 30 cm/12 in square. Cut this into 4 × 15 cm/6 in squares, boil for 3 minutes and dry on double-thick absorbent kitchen paper. Place an aubergine sandwich in the middle of each square and fold the pasta over it to make a neat parcel. Repeat with the remaining pasta and aubergines.

Set the oven at 180°C/350°F/Gas 4. Heat any remaining olive oil. Add the onions and cook for 15–20 minutes, until softened. Spread the onions in the base of an ovenproof dish. Top with the tomatoes and season well. Arrange the aubergine parcels on top, with the ends of the pasta dough underneath. Dot the tops of the parcels with the soft cheese, spreading it slightly. Mix the bread-crumbs and parmesan, then sprinkle some over the top of each parcel. Cover with greased foil and bake for 20 minutes, then remove the foil and cook for a further 10 minutes.

RIGHT
A traditional shuttered house in Tuscany.

Cannelloni with Carrot and Courgette

SERVES 4

⅓ quantity pasta dough (page 14)
3 tbsp olive oil
1 onion, chopped
1 garlic clove, crushed
225 g/8 oz carrots, grated
100 g/4 oz courgettes, grated
50 g/2 oz fresh white breadcrumbs
2 tomatoes, peeled and chopped
2 tbsp chopped parsley
1 tsp dried marjoram
salt and freshly ground black pepper
1 quantity Cheese Sauce (page 58)
3 tbsp dry white breadcrumbs

Roll out the pasta thinly into a 40 cm/16 in square. Cut it into 4 × 10 cm/4 in wide strips, then cut the strips across four times to make 16 squares. Bring a large pan of salted water to the boil and cook the pieces of pasta, a few at a time if necessary, for 3 minutes. Drain and rinse under cold water, then lay out on double-thick absorbent kitchen paper.

Set the oven at 180°C/350°F/Gas 4. Heat the oil in a large saucepan. Add the onion and garlic and cook for 15 minutes, until the onion is softened but not browned. Stir in the carrots and continue to cook, stirring all the time, for a further 20 minutes, or until the carrots are tender. Regulate the heat to prevent the carrots from browning. Stir in the courgettes, cook for 2–3 minutes, then remove the pan from the heat. Add the breadcrumbs, tomatoes, parsley, marjoram and seasoning to taste.

Place some of the vegetable mixture on a piece of pasta, then roll it up into a neat tube and place in the dish with the end of the roll underneath. Repeat with the remaining pasta and filling. Pour the cheese sauce over the cannelloni. Sprinkle the breadcrumbs on top and bake for 40 minutes, until golden brown.

CHAPTER SIX

PASTA COOL
The Freshest Salad Ideas

I hope the recipes in this chapter will inspire new enthusiasm for pasta salads. There seemed to be a culinary phase, no longer popular, when everyone made vast bowlfuls of either rice salad or pasta salad whenever a few friends gathered — a great idea it is too, but only if the pasta is perfectly "al dente", the other ingredients are complementary and the dressing brings the whole dish together.

I usually prefer pasta shapes in salads but I have also included a couple of ideas for noodles and spaghetti. Making a salad is a good way of using up any leftover pasta dough: cut out your own shapes using cutters or by cutting strips then squares or diamond shapes. However, avoid ragged shapes and irregular offcuts which can be rather off-putting in a salad. If you do happen to cook too much pasta for a meal, turning it into a salad makes it ideal for lunch boxes and picnics as well as a supper-time snack.

Smoked Salmon and Pasta Cocktails

This turns a comparatively small quantity of smoked salmon into an attractive starter.

SERVES 4

100 g/4 oz fresh pasta spirals

4 tbsp mayonnaise

4 tbsp soured cream

2 tbsp snipped chives

salt and freshly ground black pepper

4 endive or frisée leaves, roughly shredded

175 g/6 oz smoked salmon, shredded

2 tbsp chopped dill

grated rind of ½ lemon

dill sprigs, to garnish

4 lemon wedges, to serve

Cook the pasta in boiling salted water for 3 minutes. Drain and cool. Mix the mayonnaise, soured cream and chives with the pasta. Add seasoning to taste.

Arrange the endive or frisée in four glass dishes then divide the pasta between the dishes. Mix the smoked salmon with the dill and lemon rind, then arrange the shreds on top of the pasta. Garnish with dill sprigs. Serve lemon wedges with the cocktails so that their juice may be sprinkled over the smoked salmon.

Crab and Courgette Salad

SERVES 4

225 g/8 oz fresh pasta shapes

225 g/8 oz small, young courgettes

6 spring onions, chopped

6 basil sprigs

salt and freshly ground black pepper

2 tbsp lemon juice

2 tbsp olive oil

175 g/6 oz crab meat

4 eggs, hard-boiled

4 tbsp chopped parsley

Cook the pasta in boiling salted water for 3 minutes. Drain well and place in a bowl. Trim and coarsely grate the courgettes, then add them to the pasta with the spring onions. Use scissors to shred the basil and soft stalk ends into the salad. Sprinkle in seasoning to taste and mix in the lemon juice. Add the olive oil and mix well. Arrange the mixture in a serving dish, leaving a hollow in the middle.

Flake the crab meat. Chop the eggs and mix them with the crab. Fork in the parsley and seasoning to taste, then spoon the mixture in the middle of the pasta. Serve at once; if the salad is allowed to stand the pasta and courgettes become watery.

Ham and Avocado Salad

SERVES 4

350 g/12 oz fresh pasta shapes

2 tbsp cider vinegar

1 tsp prepared wholegrain mustard

1/2 tsp caster sugar

salt and freshly ground black pepper

6 tbsp olive oil

450 g/1 lb lean cooked ham (in one piece), cubed

2 avocados

4 tbsp snipped chives

50 g/2 oz walnuts, chopped

1 lettuce heart or 1/2 iceberg lettuce, shredded (optional)

Cook the pasta in boiling salted water for 3 minutes, then drain well. Meanwhile, mix the cider vinegar, mustard, caster sugar and seasoning in a basin. Whisk the mixture until the sugar and salt have dissolved. Gradually whisk in the oil. Turn the hot pasta into a dish and pour the dressing over it, then mix well.

Allow the pasta to cool slightly before mixing in the ham. Just before serving the salad, halve the avocados, remove their stones and quarter the halves lengthways. Remove the peel, then cut the flesh into chunks and mix them with the pasta. Mix in the chives and walnuts.

Arrange the salad on a base of shredded lettuce, if liked, and serve promptly. If the salad is allowed to stand, the avocado will discolour.

Smoked Mackerel Salad

This is simple, extremely well flavoured and delicious for lunch or a summer supper. Serve crusty bread to complement the pasta.

SERVES 4

225 g/8 oz fresh pasta shapes
50 g/2 oz butter
50 g/2 oz fresh white breadcrumbs
grated rind of 1 lemon
4 tbsp chopped parsley
150 ml/¼ pt soured cream
4 tbsp horseradish sauce
1 tsp finely chopped rosemary
4 spring onions, chopped
salt and freshly ground black pepper
4 smoked mackerel fillets, skinned and coarsely flaked
2 tomatoes, peeled and chopped (see Cook's Tip, page 26)

Cook the pasta in boiling salted water for 3 minutes, then drain it and set it aside to cool. Melt the butter in a frying pan, add the breadcrumbs and fry them, stirring often, until they are crisp and golden. Remove from the heat, stir in the lemon rind and 2 tbsp of the parsley, and leave to cool.

Mix the soured cream, horseradish sauce, rosemary and spring onions with the pasta. Toss the shapes well to coat them in the sauce, then add seasoning to taste. Lightly fork the smoked mackerel and remaining parsley into the pasta mixture, then turn the salad into a shallow dish. Garnish with a neat line of chopped tomato and a couple of lines of the fried breadcrumb mixture. Serve promptly after garnishing so that the breadcrumbs are still crisp when eaten.

COOK'S TIP

The rosemary must be finely chopped otherwise the spiky leaves are unpleasant. To make a neat garnish of breadcrumbs and chopped tomatoes, or any other fine mixture, use a large chef's knife or palette knife. Turn the garnishing mixture onto a clean board and scoop up some on the knife. Transfer the mixture to the salad on the horizontal knife blade. Hold the knife in position, then turn the blade vertically quite sharply to deposit the garnish in a neat line on the salad.

Pasta and Bean Salad

SERVES 4

225 g/8 oz spinach-flavoured fresh pasta shapes
225 g/8 oz French beans, cut into 5 cm/2 in lengths
425 g/15 oz can flageolet beans, drained
1 red onion, halved and thinly sliced
2 tbsp tarragon vinegar
1 tsp caster sugar
salt and freshly ground black pepper
1 garlic clove, crushed
6 tbsp olive oil
6 tbsp croûtons

Cook the pasta in boiling salted water for 3 minutes, then drain well. Turn the pasta into a bowl. Blanch the French beans in boiling salted water for 3 minutes, then drain them and add them to the pasta. Stir in the flageolet beans and onion, separating the pieces as you add them to the salad.

Shake the tarragon vinegar, sugar, seasoning and garlic in a screw-top jar. When the sugar has dissolved add the oil, put the top on the jar and shake again. Pour this dressing over the salad and toss well. Cover and leave until cold.

Just before serving, toss the salad well and mix in the croûtons. Do not leave the salad to stand once the croûtons are added or they will lose their crunch.

Spaghetti and Salami Salad

SERVES 4

350 g/12 oz fresh spaghetti

4 tbsp pine kernels

175 g/6 oz salami, cut in strips

50 g/2 oz black olives, pitted and sliced

425 g/15 oz can artichoke hearts, drained

2 tbsp cider vinegar

salt and freshly ground black pepper

½ tsp caster sugar

6 tbsp olive oil

4 tbsp chopped parsley

Cut the spaghetti into 5 cm/2 in lengths, then cook it in boiling salted water for 3 minutes. Drain the pasta well in a fine sieve before tipping it into a bowl; leave to cool.

Roast the pine kernels in a small, dry, heavy-bottomed saucepan until they are lightly browned, then tip them over the pasta. Add the salami, olives and artichoke hearts. Mix the cider vinegar, seasoning and caster sugar in a screw-top jar. Shake well until the sugar dissolves, then add the olive oil and shake again.

Pour the dressing over the salad and mix well. Toss the parsley in after the dressing, immediately before serving the salad.

Frankfurter Supper

SERVES 4

225 g/8 oz fresh pasta shapes or small pasta squares (page 14)

½ small onion, chopped

225 g/8 oz white cabbage, shredded

2 carrots, coarsely grated

150 ml/¼ pt mayonnaise

8 frankfurters, sliced

salt and freshly ground black pepper

4 tbsp chopped roasted peanuts

Cook the pasta in boiling salted water for 3 minutes, then drain it and allow to cool. Mix the onion, cabbage, carrots and mayonnaise. Toss the pasta and frankfurters with the cabbage mixture and seasoning. Divide between four serving bowls. Sprinkle with peanuts and serve at once, offering plenty of warmed crusty bread with the salad.

Tagliatelle Nests

These make a good first course or light lunch.

SERVES 4

350 g/12 oz fresh tagliatelle verdi

*2 tomatoes, peeled, seeded and diced
(see Cook's Tip, page 26)*

2 tbsp walnut oil

3 tbsp sunflower oil

juice of 1 lime

salt and freshly ground black pepper

1 tbsp chopped mint

225 g/8 oz rindless streaky bacon

100 g/4 oz shelled fresh peas

4 small courgettes

4 tbsp soured cream or fromage frais

mint sprigs, to garnish (optional)

Cook the tagliatelle in boiling salted water for 3 minutes, then drain well and turn into a bowl. Add the tomatoes, both types of oil, the lime juice, some seasoning and the mint. Toss well, cover and leave to cool.

Grill the bacon rashers until they are crisp, turning once. Drain them on absorbent kitchen paper and leave to cool. Cook the peas in boiling water for 15 minutes, then drain and set aside. Trim the courgettes, peel them very thinly so that they are a bright green outside, then halve them lengthways. Slice the courgettes thinly and mix them with the peas.

Divide the tagliatelle and its dressing between four plates, swirling it into nests. Top the nests with the courgette and pea mixture. Crush the crisply grilled bacon and sprinkle it over the courgette and pea mixture, then top with a little soured cream or fromage frais. Mint sprigs may be added as a garnish, if liked.

Herbed Tomato and Pasta Salad

Served with crusty bread, this makes a splendid starter or light lunch. It does, of course, rely on fresh basil for success.

SERVES 4

225 g/8 oz fresh pasta shapes

450 g/1 lb ripe tomatoes, peeled, seeded and quartered (see Cook's Tip, page 26)

6 spring onions, chopped

1 garlic clove, crushed

salt and freshly ground black pepper

4–6 tbsp olive oil

6 basil sprigs

Cook the pasta in boiling salted water for 3 minutes, drain and set aside to cool. Mix the tomatoes with the spring onions. Add the garlic, seasoning and olive oil, and mix well. Cover and set aside to marinate for 1 hour.

Toss the tomato mixture into the pasta. Use scissors to shred the basil, with the soft stalk ends, over the pasta. Mix well and serve at once.

BELOW
Fresh ingredients on display at an Italian delicatessen.

Pasta and Baked Pepper Salad

Skinning peppers is a boring task but the transformation in flavour is worth the effort. You can use any combination of peppers as regards colour. This is another salad that makes a good first course; it is also an ideal accompaniment for barbecued meat or poultry. Instead of shop-bought pasta shapes, you can use your own small pasta squares (page 14).

SERVES 4

225 g/8 oz fresh pasta shapes

2 red peppers

1 green pepper

1 yellow pepper

4 tbsp olive oil

2 tbsp chopped parsley

1 tbsp lemon juice

salt and freshly ground black pepper

50 g/2 oz can anchovy fillets, drained and chopped

2 eggs, hard-boiled and chopped

Cook the pasta in boiling salted water for 3 minutes, drain well, then transfer it to a shallow serving bowl.

Grill the peppers until they are scorched all over. This is fairly time-consuming as you have to stand and turn them to make sure that all the skin is blistered. Once the skin has lifted away from the pepper flesh it can be peeled off easily and any remains should be rubbed off under cold running water.

Dry the peppers on absorbent kitchen paper, halve them and cut out all their seeds and core. Slice the peppers across into thin strips and scatter them over the pasta. Mix the olive oil, parsley and lemon juice with seasoning to taste. Stir in the anchovies, then use a spoon to trickle this dressing evenly over the peppers and pasta. Sprinkle the chopped hard-boiled egg over and serve at once.

Mixed Pasta Salad

A good one for all those parties and picnics!

SERVES 4

225 g/8 oz pasta shapes

100 g/4 oz frozen sweetcorn

100 g/4 oz frozen peas

1 carrot, diced

4 celery sticks, diced

1 green pepper, seeded and diced

6 spring onions, chopped

2 tbsp chopped parsley

250 ml/8 fl oz mayonnaise

3 tbsp single cream

225 g/8 oz garlic sausage, roughly chopped

salt and freshly ground black pepper

Cook the pasta in boiling salted water for 3 minutes, drain well, then turn the pasta into a bowl. Place the sweetcorn, peas and carrot in a saucepan and add water to cover. Bring to the boil, add the celery and bring back to the boil, then cook for 5 minutes. Drain the vegetables and add them to the pasta. Allow to cool.

Mix in the green pepper, spring onions and parsley. Thin the mayonnaise with the cream, then toss this dressing into the salad. Lastly, lightly mix in the garlic sausage and taste for seasoning.

CHAPTER SEVEN

PASTA INTERNATIONAL
Doughs from Around the World

This is a mere sample of the ways in which pasta-like doughs are used all over the world, in kitchens as diverse as those in China or Poland. The chapter includes a few recipes for Chinese-style dim sum, some using the fine won ton dough from the opening chapter, and a selection of recipes for Chinese egg noodles. Eastern European pasta doughs are represented by a couple of different examples of dishes that highlight the way in which Italian culinary traditions have spread to other countries.

Most Oriental supermarkets sell fresh egg noodles and some may have fresh rice sticks, the pale, almost translucent, white pasta dough which may be cut finely, like spaghetti, or into wide ribbon noodles. Won ton wrappers are also sold ready rolled and cut into neat squares. All these pasta

types freeze well raw, and noodles can be cooked from frozen. So if you thought fresh pasta was limited to the shapes and colours created from the same simple flour and egg dough at the beginning of the book, then read on . . . or eat on!

Won Ton Soup

SERVES 4

225 g/8 oz minced pork

4 spring onions, finely chopped

2 button mushrooms, finely chopped

2 tbsp soy sauce

1 tsp sesame oil

½ quantity won ton dough (page 15)

1 egg, beaten

1 tbsp oil

1 boneless chicken breast, skinned and diced

2 leeks, sliced

900 ml/1½ pt good chicken stock

4 tbsp dry sherry

salt and freshly ground black pepper

Mix the pork, spring onions, mushrooms, soy sauce and sesame oil. Roll out the dough into a 37.5 cm/ 15 in square, dusting the surface with cornflour as necessary. The dough should be very thin. Cut the dough into 7.5 cm/3 in strips, then across into squares. Cover the dough with cling film.

To fill the won tons, take a square of dough and roll it again so that it is paper thin. Shape a little meat into a ball and place it in the middle of the dough square. Brush the meat with egg, then fold the dough around it and pinch it together to seal in the meat. Leave the corners of the dough hanging free. Fill all the won tons in the same way and place them on a platter or board dusted with cornflour.

For the soup, heat the oil in a saucepan. Add the chicken and leeks, and cook, stirring often, for 20 minutes, until the leek is softened and the chicken is just cooked. Pour in the stock and bring to the boil. Cover and simmer for 20 minutes. Stir in the sherry and seasoning to taste. Add the won tons to the soup, bring back to the boil and reduce the heat slightly so that it does not boil fiercely. Cook for 5 minutes. Test a won ton to make sure the filling is cooked, then ladle the soup and won tons into bowls. Serve at once.

101

Crispy Won Tons

These won tons are made in the same way as the ones which are cooked in soup; however, they are deep fried until crisp and served with a sweet and sour sauce. Offer them as a first course for a Chinese meal or serve them with plain boiled rice and a dish of stir-fried vegetables to make a delicious main course.

SERVES 4

won tons as for Won Ton Soup (page 101)
oil for deep frying
For the sauce
2 tbsp oil
1 tsp sesame oil
1 onion, halved and thinly sliced
1 green pepper, halved, seeded and thinly sliced
1 carrot, cut into fine 2.5 cm/1 in strips
4 tbsp tomato ketchup
4 tbsp soy sauce
1 tbsp sugar
2 tbsp cider vinegar
150 ml/¼ pt dry sherry
1 tsp cornflour
2 canned pineapple rings, cut in small pieces

Make the won tons as for the soup. Set them aside until the sauce is ready. Heat the oil and sesame oil in a saucepan. Add the onion, green pepper and carrot and cook for 5 minutes. Stir in the tomato ketchup, soy sauce, sugar, cider vinegar and sherry. Bring to the boil, reduce the heat and simmer for 3 minutes. Meanwhile, blend the cornflour with 2 tbsp cold water, then stir it into the sauce and bring to the boil, stirring all the time. Simmer for 2 minutes, then add the pineapple and set aside over low heat.

Heat the oil for deep frying to 190°C/375°F. Deep fry the won tons a few at a time, until they are crisp and golden. Drain them on absorbent kitchen paper. Place the won tons on a large flat dish or platter and spoon the sauce over them. Serve and eat at once.

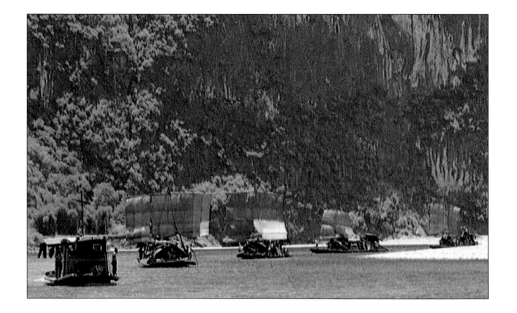

LEFT
Boats on the Li River in southern China.

Chicken Won Tons with Vegetables

These are thicker than authentic won tons. This makes them easier to handle and quicker to fill – and they taste terrific! The dim sum and vegetables make an ample complete meal; if they are served with a selection of other Chinese-style dishes, then they will yield far more portions.

MAKES ABOUT 50 – SERVES 4

4 boneless chicken breasts, skinned
¼ tsp five-spice powder
8 spring onions, chopped
1 tsp sesame oil
5 tbsp soy sauce
1 garlic clove, crushed
1 quantity won ton dough (page 15)
1 egg, beaten
3 tbsp oil
2 celery sticks, cut into fine 2.5 cm/1 in strips
1 red pepper, quartered, seeded and cut in thin strips
½ medium head Chinese cabbage, shredded
3 tbsp dry sherry

Cut the chicken into 50 small pieces. Place them in a basin and add the five-spice powder, 2 tbsp of the spring onions, sesame oil, 2 tbsp of the soy sauce and the garlic. Mix well, cover and leave to marinate for 30 minutes.

Cut the won ton dough in half. Roll out one portion into a 37.5 cm/15 in square. Cut the dough into 5 × 7.5 cm/3 in strips, then across into squares. Brush a square of dough with beaten egg. Place a piece of chicken in the middle of it, then fold the dough around the chicken and pinch it together well. Continue filling the squares, placing them on a platter dusted with cornflour as they are ready. Roll out the second portion of dough and make a further 25 won tons.

Grease a large covered dish with oil and set it to warm. Bring a large saucepan of water to the boil, then cook the won tons in batches, allowing 5 minutes when the water has come back to the boil. Drain, transfer to the dish and keep hot.

Stir-fry the vegetables while the won tons are cooking. Heat the oil in a large frying pan. Add the celery and pepper and cook, stirring, for 5 minutes. Add the remaining spring onions and cook for a further 2 minutes. Then add the Chinese cabbage and cook for 3–5 minutes. Pour in the remaining soy sauce and sherry and stir for 1 minute. Arrange the vegetables and won tons together on a platter and serve at once.

Rice Sticks with Vegetables

Egg noodles may be used instead of the rice sticks. Serve this as a light lunch or supper dish or offer it with a simple main course, such as crisp roast duck or deep-fried pork in batter.

SERVES 4

225 g/8 oz whole baby corn
2 tbsp oil
1 red pepper, seeded, quartered lengthways and thinly sliced
6 spring onions, shredded diagonally
225 g/8 oz Chinese cabbage, shredded
175 g/6 oz bean sprouts
4 tbsp soy sauce
2 tbsp dry sherry
350 g/12 oz ribbon rice sticks
4 tbsp cashew nuts, roasted
2 tbsp sesame seeds, roasted

Blanch the baby corn in boiling water for 2 minutes, then drain. Have a large pan of boiling water ready for cooking the rice sticks. Heat the oil in a wok or large saucepan. Add the pepper and spring onions, and stir-fry for 3 minutes. Add the Chinese cabbage and cook for 2 minutes before stirring in the bean sprouts. Pour in the soy sauce and sherry at the same time.

Add the rice sticks to the boiling water. Bring back to the boil and cook for 1 minute, then drain at once. By the time the rice sticks are ready, all the vegetables will be cooked. Turn the rice sticks into a serving dish or platter. Top with the vegetables and sprinkle with the cashew nuts and sesame seeds. Serve at once.

Prawn and Pork Dim Sum

MAKES 25

225 g/8 oz peeled cooked prawns, minced

100 g/4 oz minced pork

2 spring onions, finely chopped

1 tsp sesame oil

1 garlic clove, crushed

2 tsp soy sauce

½ quantity won ton dough (page 15)

1 egg, beaten

soy sauce, to serve

The prawns may be finely chopped in the food processor or liquidizer. Mix them with the pork, spring onions, sesame oil, garlic and soy sauce. Pound the mixture well so that all the ingredients bind together. Wet your hands and shape the mixture into 25 small balls.

Roll out the won ton dough into a 31 cm/12.5 in square. Dust the surface with cornflour as necessary to prevent the dough from sticking. Cut the dough into 5 × 6 cm/2½ in strips, then cut them across into squares. Brush a square of dough with a little beaten egg. Hold the dough on the palm of your hand and place a prawn ball on it. Flatten the prawn ball slightly and bring the dough up and around it, leaving the top of the mixture uncovered. Brush the dough with a little extra egg, if necessary, so that the folds cling to the side of the mixture. Shape the remaining dim sum in the same way – they should have flattened bases and the dough should be wrinkled around their sides.

Place the dim sum on a greased shallow dish which will fit in a steamer, then steam them over rapidly boiling water for 15 minutes, or until the prawn mixture is cooked. While the dim sum are cooking, prepare small dishes of soy sauce. Serve the dim sum freshly cooked: they may be dipped into the soy sauce before eating.

Mushroom Dim Sum

These are an excellent vegetarian alternative to the usual dim sum filled with pork or prawns.

MAKES ABOUT 50 – SERVES 4

4 large Chinese dried mushrooms

4 Chinese cabbage leaves

½ × 200 g/7 oz can water chestnuts, drained and chopped

4 spring onions, chopped

100 g/4 oz button mushrooms, finely chopped

1 garlic clove, crushed

2 tbsp cornflour

salt

1 egg, beaten

1 quantity won ton dough (page 15)

For the sauce

1 tbsp oil

1 tsp sesame oil

2 spring onions, chopped

15 g/½ oz fresh root ginger, peeled and finely shredded

1 celery stick, cut into fine 2.5 cm/1 in strips

1 carrot, cut into fine 2.5 cm/1 in strips

sherry (see method)

2 tsp cornflour

2 tbsp soy sauce

Place the mushrooms in a mug or very small basin. Add just enough boiling water to cover them, then put a small saucer over them and weight it down to keep the mushrooms submerged. Leave to stand for 20 minutes. Blanch the Chinese cabbage leaves in boiling water for 30 seconds, so they are just limp. Drain and squeeze all the water from them, then chop them finely.

Drain the mushrooms, reserving the soaking liquid in a measuring jug and squeezing the water from the mushrooms. Discard any woody stalks, then chop the mushroom caps and mix them with the Chinese leaves. Add the water chestnuts, spring onions, button mushrooms and garlic. Stir in the cornflour and salt to taste. Add a little beaten egg to bind the mixture, so that it clumps easily.

Prepare a large platter for the dim sum and dust it with cornflour. Cut the won ton dough in half. Roll out one portion into a 37.5 cm/15 in square, keeping the surface lightly dusted with cornflour. Cut the dough into 5 × 7.5 cm/3 in strips, then across into squares. Brush a square of dough with beaten egg, then place a little of the mushroom mixture on it. Gather the dough up around the filling to make a small bundle. Press the dough together at the top to seal in the filling. Fill all the squares of dough in the same way, then roll out the second half and repeat the process. Place the dim sum on the floured platter and cover loosely with cling film while you fill the remainder.

For the sauce, heat the oil and sesame oil together in a small saucepan. Add the spring onions, ginger, celery and carrot. Stir-fry for 2 minutes. Measure the soaking liquid from the mushrooms and add enough sherry to make it up to 300 ml/½ pt. Blend the cornflour to a smooth, thin paste with a little of the liquid, then stir in the rest of the liquid. Pour this into the pan, add the soy sauce and bring to the boil, stirring. Reduce the heat and taste for seasoning. Leave to simmer very gently.

Bring a large saucepan of salted water to the boil. Add the dim sum, bring back to the boil and cook for 5 minutes. Do not boil the water rapidly. Drain well and place in a warmed serving dish. Ladle the sauce over the dim sum and serve.

COOK'S TIP

The dim sum cook very well by steaming but this does require a lot of steamer space. Several layers of bamboo steamer, placed on a wok, are ideal and the dim sum should be placed in greased shallow dishes or on plates. If the plates are not greased the dim sum will stick.

Glossy Dumplings

Traditionally, dumplings of this type are served with a selection of other dim sum for a light lunch or mid-afternoon snack. Serve China or Jasmine tea with the dim sum.

MAKES 24

2 Chinese dried mushrooms

175 g/6 oz lean minced pork

1 tbsp finely chopped fresh root ginger

1 garlic clove, crushed

1 tsp sesame oil

2 tbsp finely chopped water chestnuts or celery

2 spring onions, finely chopped

2 tbsp soy sauce

pinch of five-spice powder

spring onion curls, to garnish

For the dough

100 g/4 oz strong plain flour

25 g/1 oz lard

To serve

1 garlic clove, finely chopped

1 tsp finely chopped fresh root ginger

1 tbsp finely chopped spring onion

1 tbsp dry sherry

about 250 ml/8 fl oz soy sauce

Place the mushrooms in a cup. Add just enough boiling water to cover them, then put a small saucer over them and weight it down to keep the mushrooms submerged. Leave to stand for 20 minutes. Mix the pork, ginger, garlic, sesame oil, water chestnuts or celery, spring onions, soy sauce and five-spice powder. Drain the mushrooms, discard any woody stalks, then chop the caps finely. Add them to the pork and mix the ingredients thoroughly.

To make the dough, place the flour in a basin. Measure 50 ml/2 fl oz boiling water and stir in the lard. When the lard has melted, pour the mixture into the flour and stir well to form a soft dough. Sprinkle a little cornflour on the work surface and knead the dough lightly, then roll it into a sausage and mark it into 24 pieces. Cut off a piece of dough to shape, then loosely cover the rest of the roll with cling film or polythene.

Knead the dough briefly into a smooth ball, then flatten it into a circle measuring about 5–6 cm/2–2½ in across. Place a little of the meat mixture in the middle, then fold the dough over it to make a tiny dumpling in the shape of a Cornish pasty. Pinch and flute the edges to seal in the filling. Grease a shallow dish or plate and place the dumpling on it. Flatten and fill the remaining dough in the same way. Steam the dumplings over boiling water for 15 minutes, until very glossy and cooked through. Test one dumpling to make sure the filling is cooked.

While the dumplings are cooking, prepare the dipping sauces: place the garlic, ginger, spring onion and sherry in four separate dishes and top up with the soy sauce. Serve the dim sum freshly cooked, garnished with spring onion curls.

COOK'S TIP

To make spring onion curls, trim the roots and some of the green of spring onions. Cut the green part and some of the white onion into fine shreds, leaving them all attached at the root end. Place in a bowl of iced water and leave for at least 30 minutes. The shredded onion curls on standing. Drain well just before using.

Crispy Chicken Chow Mein

Chow mein is a Chinese dish consisting of egg noodles mixed with other ingredients. I love this combination of textures which results from frying the noodles before topping them with sauce.

SERVES 4

4 Chinese dried mushrooms
3 boneless chicken breasts, skinned
2 tbsp cornflour
salt
350 g/12 oz Chinese egg noodles
4 tbsp oil

1 tbsp sesame oil
25 g/1 oz fresh root ginger, peeled and cut into short thin strips
4 celery sticks, cut into thin, 2.5 cm/1 in strips
1 bunch of spring onions, shredded diagonally
4 tbsp soy sauce
150 ml/¼ pt chicken stock
4 tbsp dry sherry

Place the mushrooms in a mug or small basin. Add just enough boiling water to cover them, then put a small saucer over them and weight it down to keep the mushrooms submerged. Leave to stand for 20 minutes. Drain the mushrooms, reserving the liquid, then discard any woody stems and slice the caps.

Cut the chicken into thin slices, then into fine strips. Place in a basin or polythene bag and coat with the cornflour, adding a little salt. Cook the noodles in a large pan of boiling salted water for 3 minutes. Drain well, then place the noodles in a large frying pan and lightly pat them into a flat cake; set aside.

Heat half the oil and the sesame oil in a wok or large saucepan. Add the chicken and stir-fry until the strips are lightly browned. Add the ginger, celery, spring onions and mushrooms, and cook for a further 3 minutes. Stir in the mushrooms and add the reserved soaking liquid. Pour in the soy sauce and stock and bring to the boil, stirring all the time. Leave to simmer while you cook the noodles.

Slide the noodles from the pan on to a plate. Heat the remaining oil in the pan, then slide the noodles into it. Cook until crisp and golden underneath. Use a large fish slice to turn the cake of noodles over. Alternatively, slide the noodle cake out on a plate, then invert it back into the pan. Cook the second side until crisp and golden.

Turn the noodles out on a large platter, then pour the chicken mixture over the top. Serve at once. Diners break off portions of noodles with chopsticks or a spoon and fork, taking some of the chicken mixture with the portion. The noodles soon soften in the sauce, so they must be eaten promptly.

Pork Chow Mein

Here is another way of presenting chow mein. This time, I have used Chinese five-spice powder which, even in small quantities, gives a very strong flavour.

SERVES 4

450 g/1 lb lean boneless pork, cut into very thin 2.5–5 cm/1–2 in squares
2 tsp sesame oil
1 garlic clove
2 tbsp soy sauce
6 tbsp dry sherry
pinch of five-spice powder
2 tbsp cornflour
350 g/12 oz fresh Chinese egg noodles
2 tbsp oil
1 onion, halved and thinly sliced
1 green pepper, seeded, quartered lengthways and thinly sliced
200 g/7 oz can bamboo shoots, drained and sliced
150 ml/¼ pt chicken stock

Place the pork in a basin. Add the sesame oil, garlic, soy sauce and 2 tbsp sherry. Mix in the five-spice powder, cover and leave to marinate for 2 hours.

Remove the pork from the marinade and reserve the liquid. Place the meat in a polythene bag, add the cornflour and shake the bag, holding it closed, to coat the meat evenly. Cook the noodles in boiling salted water for 3 minutes, then drain them, rinse under cold water and set aside.

Heat the oil in a wok or large frying pan. Add the pork and stir-fry over fairly high heat until the pieces are evenly and lightly browned. Stir in the onion and pepper and continue to stir-fry for 5 minutes, until the pork is well cooked and the vegetables are softened very slightly. Stir in the bamboo shoots.

Mix the remaining sherry and stock into the reserved marinade, then pour this over the meat mixture. Bring to the boil, stirring, then add the noodles to the pan and mix well until heated through. Serve at once.

Semolina Cheese Gnocchi

Gnocchi, small Italian dumplings, are usually grouped as close relatives of pasta. There are various ways of making gnocchi and using semolina is one common method.

SERVES 4

900 ml/1½ pt milk
1 bay leaf
1 mace blade
225 g/8 oz semolina
100 g/4 oz parmesan cheese, freshly grated
salt and freshly ground black pepper
2 eggs
50 g/2 oz lightly salted butter
shredded basil or chopped parsley, to serve

Pour the milk into a large pan and add the bay leaf and mace. Bring the milk slowly to the boil, then cover and remove from the heat. Allow the bay and mace to infuse for 45–60 minutes. Bring the milk back to just below boiling point, remove the bay and mace, then stir in the semolina. Cook, stirring all the time, until the mixture boils and thickens. It will become very stiff, so you have to work quite hard at stirring. This takes about 12–15 minutes.

Off the heat, beat in the parmesan cheese and seasoning. Allow the mixture to cool slightly before beating in the eggs. Grease a baking tin (a tray or roasting tin will do) and spread the gnocchi mixture out so that it is about 1 cm/½ in thick. Cover, leave until completely cold, then chill for at least a couple of hours.

Set the oven at 200°C/400°F/Gas 6. Use a little of the butter to grease an ovenproof dish. Cut the gnocchi into squares and arrange them in the dish. Melt the remaining butter and trickle it over the gnocchi, then bake for 20 minutes, until golden brown and crisp on top. Sprinkle with basil or parsley and serve at once.

Potato Gnocchi

These may be served with Meat Ragout (page 47), Good Tomato Sauce (page 56), Pesto (page 57) or Cheese Sauce (page 58). If you are looking for a simple, satisfying supper, then simply toss them with butter, freshly ground black pepper and lots of grated cheese – parmesan or another type of your choice.

SERVES 4

450 g/1 lb potatoes
25 g/1 oz butter
175 g/6 oz strong plain flour
1 tsp salt
1 egg
a little freshly grated nutmeg

Boil the potatoes in their skins until tender, about 20–30 minutes, depending on size. Drain and peel the potatoes under cold running water. Then mash them and rub the mashed potato through a fine sieve into a bowl.

Add the butter to the potato and mix well. Mix in the flour and salt, then add the egg and a little nutmeg. Mix the ingredients with a spoon at first, then use your hand to bring them together into a dough. Knead lightly until smooth.

Bring a large pan of salted water to the boil. Shape a lump of the dough into a thick sausage, then cut off small pieces, about 2.5 cm/1 in long, and indent each piece, either with your finger or with a fork. Drop the gnocchi into the boiling water, bring back to the boil and cook for 4–5 minutes. The water must not boil too rapidly and the cooked gnocchi should be firm and tender – do not overcook them or they will become soggy and watery. Use a slotted spoon to remove the gnocchi from the pan if you are cooking them in batches. Drain well and serve at once with melted butter, pepper and parmesan.

Kopytka with Kabanos

Kopytka is the Polish equivalent of potato gnocchi: exact proportions of flour to potato and egg may vary slightly but the result is unmistakably similar. Here's an idea that does not pretend to be authentic to Polish cooking but does taste good. If you cannot find kabanos, use frankfurters as an alternative.

SERVES 4

1 quantity Potato Gnocchi (page 113)
2 tbsp olive oil
2 onions, halved and thinly sliced
1 garlic clove, crushed
1 tbsp caraway seeds
4 kabanos (about 225 g/8 oz), sliced
450 g/1 lb sauerkraut, drained and shredded
salt and freshly ground black pepper
150 ml/¼ pt soured cream
paprika

Make and shape the gnocchi. Heat the oil in a large frying pan. Add the onions, garlic and caraway and cook for 20 minutes, until the onions are softened. Add the kabanos and sauerkraut, then cook, stirring often, for another 20 minutes.

Meanwhile, cook the gnocchi following the recipe instructions. Add the gnocchi to the kabanos and sauerkraut. Mix well and serve at once. Top each portion with soured cream and sprinkle with paprika.

Mushroom Uska

These little examples of Polish cooking are the same shape as tortellini. I have included the traditional Polish filling of dried mushrooms as it makes the most delicious pasta. For authenticity, the uska should be served in crystal clear beetroot soup; however, they are excellent tossed with butter and pepper, soured cream or a tomato sauce.

SERVES 4

100 g/4 oz strong plain flour
salt and freshly ground black pepper
1 egg
2 dried mushrooms (Polish or Italian)
25 g/1 oz fresh white breadcrumbs
25 g/1 oz butter
1 small onion, finely chopped

Place the flour in a bowl with ½ tsp salt. Make a well in the middle, then add the egg and 1 tbsp water. Mix to form a firm dough, using a spoon at first, then knead it by hand until smooth. Wrap the dough in polythene or cling film.

Simmer the mushrooms in water to cover for 5 minutes, then drain. Boil the cooking liquor until it is reduced to 2 tbsp and set it aside. Chop the mushrooms and mix them with the breadcrumbs. Melt the butter in a small saucepan, add the onion and cook, stirring, for 5 minutes. Mix the cooked onion with the mushroom mixture, the reserved liquor and seasoning to taste.

On a lightly floured surface, roll out the dough into a 31 cm/12½ in square. Cut it horizontally into 7 strips, then cut vertically to divide each strip into 7 squares. Place a little filling on each square and brush the edges of the dough with beaten egg. Fold the squares of dough in half to make triangular dumplings, sealing the edges well to enclose the filling. Wrap the long side of each triangle around the tip of your finger and pinch their corners together.

Bring a large saucepan of salted water to the boil. Add the uska and bring the water back to the boil. Cook for 3 minutes. Drain and serve at once.

Kopytka with Kabanos.

CHAPTER EIGHT

PASTA FOR DESSERT
Sweet Dishes to Delight

Finally, a few thoughts on sweet pasta. Depending on your culinary traditions, you will find this chapter an unexpected pleasure or simply a mere sample of the recipes that may be created.
Fruit dumplings, dusted with icing sugar and served with soured cream, are classic examples of the treats from Eastern Europe where they are eaten as a light meal in their own right. From Italy come fruit compotes

and sauces to serve with pasta. Then there are the contemporary creations, such as flavoured doughs.
If you plan to serve a substantial dessert, make the main course a light one – or simply indulge in a mid-afternoon meal instead of lunch one day and make a selection of sweet filled pasta!

Hidden Plums

Fruit dumplings of this type, encased in a dough made of potato and boiled as for ravioli, are typical of Eastern European cooking. Keep the main course simple and light when serving these for dessert as they are quite filling.

SERVES 4

450 g/1 lb potatoes
50 g/2 oz strong plain flour
1 egg
12 firm plums
75 g/3 oz white marzipan
50 g/2 oz unsalted butter
icing sugar for dredging
300 ml/½ pt soured cream

BELOW
*Villagers from Dzianisz, Poland,
returning from church.*

Boil the potatoes in their skins for 20 minutes, or until tender. Drain and peel them, then rub them through a fine sieve. Mix in the flour. Make sure the mixture is not too hot for the egg before mixing it in to make a dough. Knead the dough together, then cut it into 12 equal portions. Keep the dough covered when you are not working with it.

Slit the plums down one side and remove their stones. (If the stones do not come out easily you will have to halve the plums, but this is less successful.) Divide the marzipan into 12 small pieces and place a little in the middle of each plum. Flatten a portion of dough, place a plum on it, then knead it around the fruit to enclose it completely. Pinch the dough to seal it well.

Bring a large saucepan of water to the boil. Melt the unsalted butter and set it aside over very low heat to keep hot without cooking. Add the plums and cook for 3–5 minutes, drain them well, then turn them into a heated serving dish. Pour the butter over and dredge the plums thickly with icing sugar. Serve immediately, offering soured cream with the hidden plums.

Rum and Raisin Shapes

SERVES 6

50 g/2 oz raisins, chopped

25 g/1 oz candied peel, finely chopped

100 g/4 oz ground almonds

2 tbsp icing sugar

8 tbsp rum

⅔ quantity pasta dough (page 14)

1 egg, beaten

175 g/6 oz crab apple jelly

4 tbsp unsweetened apple juice

*2 tbsp finely chopped candied orange peel,
to decorate*

Greek-style yogurt or cream, to serve

Mix the raisins, candied peel, almonds and icing sugar. Stir in enough of the rum to bind the ingredients together; the rest of the rum is required for the glaze.

Roll out, cut and fill the pasta as for Spiced Apricot Rounds (page 123). When all the pasta is filled, cook in boiling water for 5 minutes and drain well. To make the glaze, gently heat the crab apple jelly with the apple juice until the jelly melts. Bring to the boil, then remove from the heat and stir in the remaining rum.

Serve the pasta coated with the apple glaze. Sprinkle with the chopped candied orange peel and offer Greek-style yogurt or cream with the pasta.

Plum and Blackberry Compote

A good autumnal sauce for serving with plain home-made pasta. Remember that dessert pasta looks more attractive if it is stamped out in pretty shapes using aspic cutters.

SERVES 6

100 g/4 oz sugar
grated rind and juice of 1 orange
150 ml/¼ pt dry cider
1 cinnamon stick
2 cloves
450 g/1 lb plums, halved and stoned
450 g/1 lb blackberries

Place the sugar, orange rind and juice, cider, cinnamon and cloves in a large saucepan. Heat gently, stirring, until the sugar melts. Allow the syrup to infuse over very low heat for 15 minutes, then bring it to simmering point and add the plums.

Poach the plums gently for 3 minutes, then add the blackberries and cook for 2 minutes. (Do not overcook the fruit until it becomes soft; the cooking time for the plums varies according to their texture.) Ladle this fruit sauce over the pasta, removing the spices as you do so.

119

Chocolate Bows with White Chocolate Sauce

The unusual combination of the pasta texture and sweet flavour may not be to everyone's liking but chocolate fans will approve.

SERVES 4

⅓ quantity pasta dough (page 14)
2 tbsp cocoa powder
3 tbsp icing sugar
1 tbsp walnut oil
1 tsp natural vanilla essence
225 g/8 oz white chocolate
3 tbsp golden syrup
25 g/1 oz unsalted butter
50 g/2 oz walnuts, chopped

Make the pasta dough, adding the cocoa and icing sugar to the flour before mixing in the egg and using 1 tbsp walnut oil and the vanilla essence instead of the olive oil. Roll out the dough into a 30 cm/12 in square.

Cut the dough into 3 cm/1½ in strips, then cut them across into 3 cm/1½ in squares. Pinch the opposite corners of a square of dough together, pleating the dough in the middle of the square and pressing it firmly, to make a small bow with pointed ends. Set the bow aside on a surface dusted with icing sugar. Do not cover the bows.

Before cooking the bows, prepare the white chocolate sauce. Break the chocolate into squares and place in a heatproof basin. Add the golden syrup and butter, then stand the bowl over a small saucepan of barely simmering water. Stir until the chocolate melts and the sauce is smooth. Turn the heat off and set the pan and bowl aside.

Cook the bows in just-boiling water for 3 minutes. Meanwhile, pour some chocolate sauce on warmed plates. Drain the bows, then arrange them on the sauce. Sprinkle with nuts and serve at once.

Chocolate Fruit Dreams

SERVES 6

*⅓ quantity plain pasta dough (page 14) or
1 quantity chocolate pasta dough
(see Chocolate Bows, page 120)*

225 g/8 oz strawberries, sliced

6 tbsp maple syrup

225 g/8 oz raspberries

300 ml/½ pt double or whipping cream, whipped

2–3 tbsp toasted chopped hazelnuts

Make the pasta dough, roll it into a 30 cm/12 in square and cut it into 2.5 cm/1 in strips. Cut the strips at an angle to make diamond shapes (rather like cutting marzipan leaves when decorating a cake). Cook the pasta in boiling water for 3 minutes, then drain it well.

In a bowl, mix the sliced strawberries with the maple syrup. Add the drained pasta and mix lightly. Mix the raspberries with the pasta and strawberries, taking care to keep them whole. Divide the fruit and pasta between 6 dishes. Top with generous swirls of cream, then sprinkle with toasted chopped hazelnuts. Serve at once.

Spiced Apricot Rounds

SERVES 6

225 g/8 oz ready-to-eat dried apricots, finely chopped

1 tsp ground cinnamon

2 tbsp icing sugar

grated rind and juice of 1 orange

⅔ quantity pasta dough (page 14)

1 egg, beaten

100 g/4 oz clear honey

50 g/2 oz flaked almonds, toasted

1 tsp cinnamon or allspice

orange slices, to decorate

whipped cream, to serve

Mix the apricots, cinnamon or allspice, icing sugar and orange rind. Cut the dough in half and roll out one portion into a 30 cm/12 in square. Use a 5 cm/2 in round fluted cutter or a shaped cutter to stamp out pieces of dough. If you work neatly you will get 36 shapes.

Brush a piece of dough with egg, place a little of the apricot mixture in the middle, then cover with a second piece of dough. Pinch the edges together firmly to seal in the filling. Continue until all the shapes are used, then repeat with the second portion of dough. Place the finished rounds on a lightly floured plate and keep them loosely covered while you are filling the remaining shapes.

Bring a large saucepan of water to the boil and cook the pasta in batches for 5 minutes each. Drain well. While the pasta is cooking, heat the orange juice and honey. Serve the hot pasta coated with the honey and orange juice and sprinkled with the toasted flaked almonds. Decorating individual plates with attractive pieces of sliced orange improves the appearance of the dessert. Serve with whipped cream.

Summer Fruit Sauce

Serve this sauce with pasta shapes, either bought or home-made. Instead of pouring the sauce over the pasta, ladle the sauce into dishes then top it with pasta and sprinkle with chopped nuts and icing sugar.

SERVES 4

225 g/8 oz redcurrants

75 g/3 oz sugar

juice of 1 orange

225 g/8 oz strawberries, halved

225 g/8 oz raspberries

mint sprigs, to decorate

Place the redcurrants, sugar and orange juice in a saucepan. Heat gently until the sugar dissolves, then bring to the boil. Cook gently for 1 minute, then remove from the heat.

Mix the strawberries and raspberries into the redcurrants. Add the mint sprigs, if liked, and mix lightly, then pick them out to use as a decoration when serving the sauce.

LEFT
Spiced Apricot Rounds.

GLOSSARY

Agnolotti A name sometimes used for round filled pasta (see Ravioli).

Al Dente The Italian term used to describe the texture of pasta which is perfectly cooked: tender but not soft, with a bit of bite or resistance.

Bain Marie A container of hot water in which to stand a dish during baking. The outer container of water protects the contents of the dish from fierce heat which may spoil delicate foods, such as custards or light mixtures set with egg. A bain marie may also be used on the hob.

Bamboo Shoots Oriental ingredient sold prepared in cans. Canned bamboo shoots may be packed in large, semi-circular chunks or cut into fine slices. They may be used in a wide variety of dishes, including chow mein.

Basil Fragrant, full-flavoured herb with large, bright green, tender leaves. The leaves bruise easily, losing texture and some of their flavour in chopping, so they are best shredded using scissors. The soft stalk ends may also be finely snipped and used. The flavour of basil diminishes on cooking, so it is usually added late in the preparation of a dish. The flavour of dried basil does not compare well with that of the fresh herb so it is best avoided in this form. Buy growing pots or plant a large potful outside in summer months. Preserve any excess by making pesto (page 57).

Bay Leaves Evergreen shrub of laurel family. The leaves have a distinct flavour which is excellent in many savoury dishes and some sweet puddings. Bay leaves also freeze well or the dried herb may be used.

Bean Sprouts Sprouted mung beans, harvested when the shoots are about 2.5–5 cm/1–2 in long and still white. They are crunchy and delicately flavoured, and may be used raw or very lightly cooked in a wide range of dishes including chow mein. Mung beans may be sprouted by first soaking overnight in cold water, then draining and keeping moist in a part-covered jam jar for 2–3 days. The beans must be rinsed with water every day and kept in a warm place so that they germinate. The jar may be covered with a piece of white cotton, kept in place with an elastic band.

Bows Another name sometimes used for butterfly pasta shapes. You can make these by hand, by cutting small squares of thinly rolled pasta and pinching or twisting each one in the middle.

Cannelloni Dried cannelloni are wide tubes about 10 cm/4 inch long; however, fresh cannelloni are made by cutting sheets of pasta and rolling them around the filling.

Cardamoms An aromatic, mild spice. The small pale green pods consist of a papery covering which conceals compartments filled with small black seeds. The whole pods are added to dishes and they may be chewed. They have a refreshing, zesty, lemon-ginger flavour which is used in both savoury and sweet cooking.

Chestnut Mushrooms See Mushrooms.

Chick Peas Small round dried pulses, pale cream in colour with indented sides. They require soaking overnight before boiling in water for about 50 minutes, or until tender; alternatively, canned chick peas have an excellent texture. Their nutty flavour is good with pasta and their high protein content is valuable in main dishes.

Chillies There are many types of chillies, varying in hotness, from extremely fiery types to mild chillies. The small, wiry chillies are often very hot; canned jalapeño chillies are fairly mild. As well as heat, chillies have a distinct peppery flavour which is most apparent in the milder types. The seeds are especially hot, so cut out the core and rinse away all seeds before use. Always wash your hands after handling chillies as their juices are highly irritating, causing an excruciating, burning sensation when in contact with sensitive areas, such as eyes, or any grazed skin or cuts.

Chinese Dried Mushrooms Although several types of dried fungus are used in Chinese cooking, this term refers to dried shiitake mushrooms. The cap, which varies in size from 2.5–7.5 cm/1–3 inch, is dark outside and the stalks are usually very woody. They have a slightly musty flavour which adds a rich, distinctive characteristic to oriental dishes. They must be soaked for at least 15 minutes, then drained and the stalks removed before cooking. The soaking liquor is often used to flavour sauces.

Chinese Egg Noodles Fine round noodles made from a rich egg dough. Available fresh from oriental supermarkets, these freeze extremely well. The noodles cook in 1–2 minutes in boiling water, slightly longer if frozen.

Chinese Leaves Tall, crinkly and closely packed vegetable, almost a cross between a cabbage and a lettuce. The pale green leaves have a wide white central "vein" which is crisp and crunchy to eat. May be shredded and used raw or lightly cooked.

Chives Herb which resembles fine round grass, this has an onion-like flavour. Snip into very short lengths using scissors instead of chopping.

Chow Mein A Chinese noodle dish. The noodles may be soft or they may be shallow fried after cooking until partly crisped.

Cider Vinegar Vinegar prepared from an apple base, this is less harsh than malt vinegar or wine vinegar.

Cinnamon Sweet spice used in savoury and sweet cooking. Obtained from the bark of a tree, cinnamon is sold as sticks, which is the rolled bark stripped of the rough outer covering, or ground. Cinnamon is also available as rough pieces of unstripped bark. Sticks and bark are removed from dishes before eating.

Coconut Milk Made by soaking coconut flesh in boiling water, then draining and squeezing out all the liquid. Fresh or unsweetened desiccated coconut may be used. However, it is easier to buy instant coconut milk in powder form. Creamed coconut, sold as blocks or cans, may also be melted or diluted in hot water to make coconut milk. Instant powder is most convenient and it has the longest shelf life before the packet is opened.

Coriander Aromatic spice with mild flavour. Small round, pale seeds about the size of peppercorns which may be crushed, or ready ground types are available.

Coriander Leaves Fresh herb grown from coriander seeds, this resembles flat-leafed parsley in appearance but it has a strong flavour.

Croûtons Small cubes or shapes of fried bread, used as a garnish or to add a contrast in texture to dishes.

Cumin Small, slim, oval seeds with a distinct flavour; usually white (creamy, in fact) although black seeds are also available. Ground cumin has a strong flavour.

Curry Powder A mixture of spices, including fenugreek, coriander, cumin, cinnamon, chilli powder, turmeric and cloves. Curry powder is a British invention to use instead of mixing individual spices to achieve a specific flavour in a dish, which is authentic to Indian cooking. When buying curry powder, look for a good-quality brand with a mild flavour and it is useful for pepping up Western-style dishes.

Dates, fresh These have firm flesh and a papery skin which is easily rubbed or peeled off. Halve the dates or slit them down one side to remove the long thin stones. Good with goat's cheese: slice them and toss them with crumbled goat's cheese and pasta for a delicious light meal.

Dill Feathery herb which resembles fennel in appearance but bears no relationship flavour-wise. Fresh dill has a delicate, distinctive flavour which is excellent with seafood or eggs. Dried dill is so inferior that it is not worth using: it has a "green" taste that somehow imparts a grass-like image to a dish. Freeze fresh dill for use in sauces; use from frozen.

Dim Sum Chinese snacks, including little dumplings made from a pasta-like dough.

Dolcelatte A creamy blue cheese of the Gorgonzola family but far milder. Delicious with pasta, either gently melted into warm cream to make a rich sauce or diced and tossed with hot, buttery pasta.

Dried Mushrooms Boletus or cep (or porcini in Italian) are available dried in slices or smaller pieces. They are soaked before use and the soaking water should be retained to flavour sauces. There are other types of dried mushroom to be found in delicatessens, some strung up whole. They have a strong flavour, so are used in small quantities.

Endive In British cookery this is a frilly, firm-texture lettuce-like vegetable; in American the term is used for chicory.

Fettucine Ribbon noodles, also known as tagliatelle.

Five-spice Powder A Chinese spice which is extremely strong. As its name implies, the powder consists of five spices, including star anise, cloves, cinnamon, fennel and anise pepper. Use this sparingly.

Flageolet Beans Small, oval, pale green pulses. They have a delicate flavour which goes well with pasta. Buy dried and soak overnight, then boil them for about 45 minutes or use canned. Good also with lamb, mint and pasta.

Frisée Another name for endive or curly endive, the frilly lettuce.

Fromage Frais Fresh, un-ripened cheese which is soft and creamy. May be used instead of cream but it curdles quickly on heating, so should not be allowed to approach simmering point in a sauce. Various fat levels are available, from virtually fat-free to rich, creamy fromage frais with a high fat content.

Ginger, fresh root Knobbly root which has a beige skin. When young, the skin is thin and the flesh zesty and tender. Older, tough ginger which is wrinkled and softened is not worth buying. The flavour is slightly lemony and slightly hot – but large quantities of fresh ginger have to be used before a hot flavour is imparted to a dish.

Gnocchi A type of pasta made from soft dough, shaped into small pieces and boiled. Semolina or potato may be used as the base; or a dough of ricotta cheese and spinach may be shaped into gnocchi.

Jalapeño Chillies See chillies.

Lasagne Wide strips or squares of pasta.

Mace Spice which forms a net-like covering around nutmeg. It is available dried in orange-coloured pieces, known as blades, or ground. Good with duck, game, meat and sausage-meat.

Marjoram Sweet herb with a distinct flavour that is typical of Mediterranean dishes. Fresh or dried may be used, the fresh herb has a mild flavour.

Mint Familiar herb which is best fresh or frozen as the dried type has a slightly inferior flavour.

Mozzarella Cheese Small round cheeses with a rubbery texture and delicious creamy, very mild flavour. They are un-ripened. Traditionally made from buffalo milk. Buy only Italian mozzarella as it is superior to some other types (for example, Danish mozzarella has an inferior flavour and texture). Used in salads, as a pizza topping and for baking on pasta dishes.

Mushrooms There are many types; however, the familiar fresh mushrooms also vary. Button mushrooms or closed button mushrooms that are very small are ideal for cooking whole or halved. They are pale and mild in flavour. Closed cap mushrooms which are slightly larger and nominally darker in colour are ideal for slicing. Field mushrooms or open cap mush-rooms are dark with large caps. They may be stuffed or grilled, or sliced for using in a dark sauce as they have a good flavour. However they discolour a pale sauce.

Chestnut mushrooms are medium in size with closed caps which are brown rather than beige in colour. They have a slightly stronger flavour than ordinary button or closed cap mushrooms.

Oyster mushrooms are soft, pale and delicate. They are large flat, fan-shaped caps which are delicate in appearance and flavour. They should be cooked briefly, by poaching or sauté-ing. They are ideal in a mixed mushroom dish.

Nutmeg Hard, round nut which is grated on a small grater. The spice has a sweet, strong flavour which is valued in sav-oury and sweet cooking. Good with cheese and in milk sauces.

Olive Oil An essential adjunct to fresh Italian pasta. Whole books have been devoted to olive oil as there is so much to say about the production and quality of the ingredient. In brief, oils vary significantly: dark green extra virgin olive oil is taken from the first pressing of the olives. It has a rich flavour which is delicious with garlic and par-mesan cheese to dress fresh pasta. Lighter coloured oil which is taken from successive press-ings has less flavour. Most super-markets offer a range of qual-ities, price and colour being a good indication of flavour, and superior varieties are sold in some delicatessens. It is worth buying a small bottle of rich olive oil if you like the flavour – smell the oil and you will notice the difference before you taste the sweetness in its flavour. Average quality olive oil is fine for cook-ing; look for a mixture of olive and sunflower oil if you find the flavour of olive oil alone rather overpowering.

Oregano Wild marjoram, a strongly flavoured herb which is good with most pasta dishes. Dried may be used instead of fresh.

Paglia e Fieno Narrow spinach (verdi) and white noodles com-bined, the Italian name means straw and hay.

Parmesan Cheese Strong, hard cheese which should be bought in a chunk, then grated as required. Alternatively, pro-cess chunks of parmesan in a food processor until fine, then freeze and remove small amounts as required. Fresh par-mesan has a sweet flavour which cannot be compared with the harsh odour and strong tang of dry, grated parmesan which is sold in tubs.

Parsley Familiar herb which is available fresh all year; chop a large batch and freeze to use from frozen.

Pasta Shapes, fresh There is a limited variety of manufactured (extruded) shapes available in fresh pasta, including spirals or twists and penne as well as the usual spaghetti, noodles and paglia e fieno. Make your own unorthodox alternatives by cutting rolled pasta dough into small squares or shredding it into oblong pieces.

Penne Or quills, these are short, narrow tubes with ends cut at a slant.

Peppercorns Dried peppercorns are available as widely used black or less often white, both of which give a better flavour when used freshly ground. Dried green peppercorns are lighter and easily crushed. Red or pink peppercorns are similar in size but they are not of the same family. Pickled green peppercorns are available in brine. Fresh green peppercorns are also available occasionally, sold on their stalks: they have a strong but refreshing pepper flavour.

Pine Kernels Small oval, pale cream coloured seeds which have a nutty flavour. They are used plain in pesto or may be roasted for use in a variety of sauces or dishes.

Pistachio Oil Bright green oil from pistachio nuts, this has a strong flavour and should be used sparingly.

Ravioli Round or square shapes of stuffed pasta, depending on the region of origin.

Rice Sticks Chinese and Japanese pasta made from rice flour. They are white in colour and may be transparent, widths range from wide ribbon noodles to very fine vermicelli. They cook quickly and have a very light flavour and texture. Available fresh from oriental supermarkets.

Ricotta Cheese A light soft cheese which differs from the ordinary cheeses in that it is made from the whey rather than the curds. It does not melt and run during cooking. Used in fillings for pasta and in gnocchi dough.

Rosemary Strongly flavoured herb with short, dark-green spikes which sprout along woody stems. Dried is quite woody in texture. Good with pork and lamb.

Sage Herb with soft, pale green leaves and a peppery flavour. Good with pork, vegetables and cheese.

Salsa A Mexican term for a spicy fresh sauce.

Sauerkraut Salted white cabbage available in jars. Squeeze out excess brine, then hold the sauerkraut in a firm bundle and slice it to form shreds.

Spaghetti Fine round strands of pasta, fresh spaghetti is sold curled in packets.

Spirals or Twists The most common fresh pasta shapes.

Sun-dried Tomatoes Available in packets, the tomatoes are easily cut up by shredding using scissors. They impart a rich flavour to dishes. Soak them in liquid or olive oil to soften (some are packed in olive oil) or simmer in a sauce.

Tagliatelle Ribbon noodles.

Tahini A beige-colour paste made from sesame seeds.

Thyme Familiar, small-leafed herb with a strong flavour. Use fresh or dried.

Tofu Also known as beancurd, this is prepared from soya beans. It is sold in blocks, displayed in chiller cabinets. The natural curd is tasteless and it readily absorbs the flavour of other ingredients with which it is cooked. Smoked or flavoured tofu is also available.

Tortellini Small stuffed pasta shapes enclosing a little filling. They are shaped by stuffing squares or rounds of pasta and sealing in a triangular shape, then pinching long ends together.

Turmeric Bright yellow spice ground from a root of the same colour. It has a distinct, mild flavour.

Walnut Oil Strongly flavoured oil which should be used sparingly as a flavouring rather than for frying. It may be used to flavour pasta dough or added to sauces.

Water Chestnuts Small, rounded and white when prepared, canned water chestnuts have a crisp texture and a light, nutty flavour. They are used in oriental cooking, usually sliced.

Won Tons Small Chinese dumplings made from a light pasta-like dough with a little filling. They may be simmered in water or stock or deep fried.

Yam Large root vegetable with a crisp, papery skin which is peeled off using a knife to reveal the white flesh which is slightly slimy when raw. Cut into pieces and boil in salted water for 10–20 minutes, depending on the size of the pieces, until tender. Drain; the vegetable is rather like very floury potatoes.

INDEX